Life

on

Parira

Rod and Ellen McKenzie

Preface

Much of the material in this book was written or dictated by Rod McKenzie. The story of his early life is recorded in a previous book called the "McKenzies of Nesscroft". Ellen McKenzie wrote about her young life and her early years at Parira.

The chapters towards the end were written by their son Ron based on his memories and information from the diaries kept by Rod, Ellen and Rod's mother. Material written by Rod is interspersed where available.

When the narrator of the history changes, the name of the writer is recorded in the section heading.

2008

Early History

The History of the Motukaika Block
(from Noel Crawford - The Station Years)

The 20,000 acre Cannington Run No 59 was taken up by Henry Knight in 1856 when aged 20. He had come from Cannington near Bridgewater in Somerset. He had brought money from England, probably loaned by his Father. The land was leasehold and his rental for 1857 was £19. In 1864 Knight sold the land between the Motukaika and White Rock River to David Innes the owner of the adjacent Pareora run. The boundary with Levels Station was fenced on the Levels side of the Pareora River.

The same year David Innes took on Edward Elworthy as partner and manager. The following year Edward Elworthy bought out David Innes's share in the run. He renamed the run Holme Station. For many years two shepherds based at the Motukaika outstation (where Rowleys lived) were responsible for the stock work on the west of the Station.

At the end of 1904, after Edward Elworthy had died, the trustees of his estate sold the 7,593 acres which lay between the Motukaika and White Rock rivers to Simon Mackenzie and James Scott, land dealers, who at various times had owned several stations and subdivisions of stations in South Canterbury. They paid £4-14-0 an acre for the bulk of the land that was mainly arable and £2-10-0 an acre for the tussock-land at the western end (which became the Longridge property), a total of about 28,000 acres. During the year that Scott and Mackenzie owned the block, they built a substantial woolshed on the eastern end, at the site of the old Motukaika outstation. In December 1905, they sold the land to Richard, Thomas, and John Belcher, and Robert Chapman, who were all of Christchurch for £6 an acre for the arable land and about £3 an acre for the tussock block. The precise area, and therefore value, of the latter was not known, and became the subject of a lengthy court case between the speculating parties.

The Belchers and Chapman immediately made plans for subdividing the Motukaika block; in January 1906 they had it surveyed into eleven farms, each being a former paddock of Elworthy's. They sold most of these farms over the next three years at a price that was generally some 50 per cent more than they had paid.

Gainsford Family

Mr Gainsford was the first owner of Parira. He was born in 1876 in Middlesex, where his family owned a market garden, from which they supplied the Covent Garden market with fruit and vegetables.

His grandfather and uncle came to Christchurch in 1882. His own family came to Christchurch on a sailing ship the following year. They did not see any land from the day they left the London docks until they arrived in Lyttleton, 100 days later. The uncle killed a pig for Christmas and it was the only fresh meat they had on the trip. Most of the time, they had to depend on the supplies that they could buy on the ship. There were huge casks of saltbeef on board, from which a ration was weighed out for each person every day.

His grandfather had a market garden, glass house and fruit and vegetable shop in Victoria Street in Christchurch. He went out of business when a fire destroyed the shop. Mr Gainsford's father milked dairy cows at Burwood, Styx, Sumner, St Albans, Innes Road and then Fendalton. He supplied a dairy operated by his mother. They were a large family: seven boys and five girls.

His older brother Arthur drowned in the Avon River near Burwood and his younger sister died of diphtheria aged nine. Another sister would have drowned at Fendalton when she fell in the river, if his father had not jumped in and pulled her out. His father gave up dairying after being sick with typhoid.

Mr Gainsford helped to milk the cows while attending school in Christchurch. After leaving school, he worked on farms in North Canterbury. He first took up land near Hawarden, where he ran sheep and grew crops. He married Mary Hogben of Masons Flat. When the Motukaika block was being cut up by Messrs Belcher and Chapman in 1906, he purchased the bare land for £10 an acre.

> They grew large areas of wheat, developed good flocks and ran cattle. All the agricultural work was done with a team of horses, which made it necessary to grow large crops of oats for chaff. Some was always threshed, the oats sold to the Timaru mills and the straw used on the farm. The threshing and chaff cutting was all done by the Winter family (Allister Evans, The Silver Tussock, p 117).

Building the House (Rod)
After buying the farm, Mr Gainsford came in a horse and dray and put up a tent in the corner on the site of the current house. Most of the farm was in stubble, as the previous owners had been leasing

large blocks out each year for cash cropping. He lived in the tent while he built a shed over it. He later built three rooms of the house. Over the years he completed the house and sheds, put up fences and dug wells for water.

Mr Gainsford was a good man but had a sad life. His wife was a very negative lady (not surprising given the tough life). Mrs Gainsford was a Catholic. He would take her to church every week, but would wait outside in the gig. Later he started going in with her.

His family also caused him a lot of grief. Evelyn married Pat Casey, who was a muddler of a farmer. The roof of his mouth was missing and he could not talk properly. They had a huge family in a tiny house and she struggled to make ends meet all her life.

Mary was suddenly crippled. The cause was never found, but some people said it was the result of a frightening experience. She married Mick Casey and had four children, but she spent most of her life in bed. Mick had to let his brother Gerald take over the farm so they could move to Timaru. He started a fruit shop under the Crown Hotel, which was owned by his family. They struggled all their lives.

The youngest daughter Eileen went to the West Coast and married John Shanahan, who owned a shop and was supposed to be wealthy. He turned out to be an alcoholic and owned nothing. In the end, she left him.

Young Bill was a bit of a rebel. He would go and board with Granny McKenzie over the holidays, because he was unhappy at home. He bought a motor bike and would go out with the district hoons, Eddie Kelynack, Jim Kelynack and Jack Williams. This was fairly harmless stuff, but it really upset his father. A Scottish girl on the farm where he worked got pregnant and he had to marry her. This brought more disappointment to his father. Bill later farmed successfully in Taiko.

After selling the farm, Mr Gainsford moved back to Christchurch. He soon got bored with retirement and bought another farm in North Canterbury. He died in 1971.

Chris Cooper

The farm next door to Parira was first owned by Mr Gainsford's brother, who had arrived at the same time as his brother. He had five children. When his wife died, he lost interest in the farm. He was a good friend with Mr Butterworth who lived over the river. They would get together every day and just sit and smoke and talk. A track was worn through the riverbed where they walked across each day.

Chris Cooper bought the farm when he returned from the first war. He paid 20 pounds an acre, which soon proved to be far too much. Life was always a struggle for him. He had "trench feet" from standing in water and could not walk properly. His wife died in childbirth, so he had to look after the five children himself.

He had to keep his horses in the Swamp Paddock. They seemed to get a lot of worms from drinking swamp water and were always dying.

The farm was only 200 acres, so it was too small to be economic. He could not afford lime, so his crops were always poor and full of weeds. He was eventually sold up by the bank. Chris would have been left with nothing, after struggling for many years (and serving his country).

Jim Calder

Jim Calder paid $18 an acre for the farm, but he was a poor farmer. He bought a header and got into growing small seeds. He and Jock Blackmore had the only two headers in the district. Jock was really careful and would not work until the header was running perfectly. Jim Calder was just the opposite. People would joke that his favourite weapon was the hammer, because he was always banging away at the header. He did some heading for me, but he never got it right. The screenings would be going into the bag while the wheat was going out on the ground.

Jim was hopeless with machinery, but he was really good with dogs and horses. I first saw what good working dogs could do by watching him and I eventually took over his mustering beat at Nimrod.

Jim Calder had two daughters. His wife died of cancer before they had started at school. He then started drinking and went downhill badly.

He sold the farm to Mr Robins in 1949 when Ronald was a baby. When Arnold Wilson came down to the clearing sale, he bought Miss Wilson down to visit Ellen. Most people in the district thought she was a bit odd, but she really enjoyed nursing Ronald, so Ellen saw a different side of her.

Mr Robins

Mr Robins started farming when he was about sixty years old. He had been a cabinetmaker and beekeeper. He had always wanted to farm, but his wife had refused to go with him, because she did not want to live in the country. Eventually, he decided to go on his own. His wife stayed in Temuka, and he would drive up to the farm most days to work. He only stayed there when he was really busy.

Mr Robins didn't know much about farming when he started and he would often turn up with a sheep in trouble for me to sort out. The farm was probably uneconomic, but he made a living from his bees.

Finding a Wife

I really wanted to get married and could not imagine being married to a girl that didn't go to church. None of the girls that I knew went to church. I prayed that God would bring a "church girl" across my path and soon this teacher arrived. I must have been getting better at praying by then.

Ellen Cleland came and boarded at Riverbank in 1942. The male teacher, who had been boarding with us, went overseas to the war and she came as a relieving teacher until a permanent appointment could be made. We had heard that the next teacher would be a woman and I was against boarding her, because I had not had a happy experience with female teachers at school. I thought that they were all dragons. Helen was determined that she would come and in the end, she and Mum won the day.

I was up at Campbell's working on the harvest when she arrived, so I did not see her. By the time I got home late at night, she was already in bed. I was away again early in the morning before she came out.

Each night, Mum and Helen would talk about what a lovely girl the teacher was, so I thought that I had better check it out, so I made an excuse to go home early from harvesting for my meal to have a look at her. I got a surprise when I saw her, because she did not look like the teachers that I had known when I was younger.

A short time later, when Helen was away, the Campbell's rang up and offered to take Ellen and me to a dance at Cave. Mum was really determined that Ellen should go, because she thought that she would not stay in the district, if she did not get to know people, so we went to the dance.

It was funny, because Jim Campbell would usually drive the car, but on this occasion, his younger brother Jack had taken charge and was driving the car. We set off up the road with Jim and Jack in the front and Jean Campbell and Ellen and I were in the back. Going around the school corner, Jack drove too wide and went off the road on the left-hand side, tipping us all in a heap in the back of the car.

When we were coming home, I expected Jack to go down over Martin's Crossing and drop us off at Riverbank, but he just drove straight to his own home over the Cliffs Bridge. Petrol was really short at that time, so I said that if he stopped at his place, we would walk home. We got to walk home together and that was the first time that I got to talk to Ellen alone.

I had a real inferiority complex and thought that if a girl knew about what had happened to Dad, she would not want anything to do with me. I assumed that Ellen did not know, but her Uncle Bob had already told her everything.

Helen did not like us being together and tried to keep us apart. On a Sunday, we would be sitting talking on the seat that Uncle Jack built at the front of the house. Helen came out every few minutes to shake a mat. She was checking to see what we were doing, but I don't know what she thought we could get up to.

Ellen was only there for a short time, before she got a permanent job at Pleasant Point. It was a much better position for her. I would ride or bike over to Totara Valley each Sunday to see her.

I believed that Ellen was an answer to my prayers, so in the following February, I asked her to get engaged and she accepted. She was a little surprised, because she would have been happy to carry on being friendly for longer. I was worried that someone might come along and head me off. She did not seem to worry about what had happened to my father.

Growing Up
(Ellen)

Growing Up

Looking back over my life, I am thankful I grew up in a large family. I was born at a maternity home called Whare Nana in Timaru on August 25th 1920 to Margaret and Andrew Cleland, their sixth child and fourth daughter. I remember very little of my pre-school years, but I presume they were happy ones. During those years, my brother Jim was born in 1922 and my sister Mary in 1924. They became my playmates in my younger childhood years.

I have very little recollection of my first years at school. I began at the beginning of the third term of 1925 at Totara Valley school. Miss Thompson was the sole-charge teacher. At that time our family drove to school in a gig with a horse named Mischief. My brother Leslie being the oldest boy in the group attending Totara Valley School would be the driver. I can remember sitting on the floor of the gig with Lloyd, because only Les, Margaret and Jessie could fit on the seat.

When I started my schooling, my eldest sister Sadie had already commenced her secondary schooling as a boarder at Timaru Girls High School. Margaret followed in her footsteps the next year and Les the following year after that.

As I advanced through my schooling, I remember more about the games we played and the pupils that attended Totara Valley than about the schoolwork. One thing that stands out is reading aloud to the class from the School Journal, which did have good stories. In the playground, we were like one big family playing games together. We did experience one or two bossy ones who liked to have their own way and would argue until they got it.

Two popular games were Bye the Door and Basketball. Sometimes our basketball team played matches against teams from other sole-charge schools.

One unusual happening that stands in my memory was when one of the horses pushed open the school gate and all the horses got out of the horse paddock and went home. After school, we pushed and pulled our gig up the three hills as far as the Camp part of Dad's farm. We were so indignant when Mr McLeod (Norman's father) came along and wouldn't allow us to take it home.

After Les left Totara Valley to attend Timaru Boys High School and Jessie went to Timaru Girls High, we changed our way of travelling to school. My father, being a forward-looking man, sent Lloyd to the Pleasant Point District High School for his Form II year in 1931. After he left Totara Valley, Mary and I rode the old horse Mischief to school and Jim rode the pony Zetty. I never liked riding. Sometimes the old horse would stumble and fall. Mary and I both remember feeling embarrassed when we were passing a mill working in our paddock and we fell off. Another time we rode home in a thunderstorm.

In 1932 I was going into Form I, so Dad sent me to the Point School. To go to Point, I had to walk down Cleland's zigzag to the Fairlie main road where I caught the passenger bus that travelled from Fairlie to Timaru. After school, we caught the bus by Mr Gosling's fruit shop at 4.15 p.m. It cost half a crown (25c) to travel on the bus for a week. I needed a while to adapt after being in a one-teacher school, but I did enjoy being in a larger school.

During my first year at Point, I was taught by the principal Mr de Montalk, who later shifted to Fiji. I was a friend of his daughter and she sent me some coral and shells from the beach there. Our children later enjoyed taking these to school for nature study, as the other children had not seen coral.

Sudden Death

A tragic change came into our lives when our father died on 21 August 1932, at the age of 46 years. He died of blood poisoning after being in hospital for ten days. It was a hard time for our family and the younger members were told very little about Dad's sickness or his funeral. We were not able to visit Dad in hospital or say goodbye to him. I remember standing on the main road, when Uncle Bob drove him through Point on the way to hospital, but Uncle Bob did not stop and Dad did not see me. The day of his funeral I was sent with the younger members of our family to be with Beatrice Cleland at "Loudoun".

After Mum returned home (she had been staying in Timaru with Grandma Shepherd) Mary and I were sent to stay for a week with Dad's sister Aunty Mary Pringle and her husband at Cattle Valley. They did endeavour to be good to us, but Mary and I were so homesick, because we really didn't know Aunty Mary.

The year before Dad died was a very hard one. New Zealand was in the middle of the Great Depression and farm prices were very low. During 1931, South Canterbury experienced a severe drought, which didn't break until February 1932. The crops were a failure and stock had to be sold due to lack of feed. I can remember Dad carting water from the river in a tank on the back of an old truck. At our home, we were dependent on rainwater for the house. We only had a bath once a week and several of us had to use the same water.

Before I share my memories of Dad, I will include the Obituary that was in the paper after his death.

Mr Andrew John Cleland

Through the death of Mr AJ Cleland, the districts around Sutherlands, Totara Valley and Pleasant Point sustained a great loss. Mr Cleland was ever ready to assist any worthy cause and by his kindly, generous personality he endeared himself to all who came in contact with him. In the early days of settlement in South Canterbury Mr Cleland's parents took up land in the Sutherlands District and Andrew was born at their home, Loudoun on October 12th 1885. He received his schooling at Totara Valley and Sutherlands

15

schools. After leaving school, he worked on his father's farm till 1910. In this year Mr Cleland Senior retired, the farm was divided among the sons. Andrew then settled on part of the property and was married to Margaret Shepherd.

As an indication of the interest taken by Mr Cleland in things pertaining to the welfare of the community was his long service on the Totara Valley School Committee of which he was a member for the last 21 years holding the office of chairman for the last 12 years.

The Pleasant Point branch of Farmers Union owes a great deal to his organizing ability and for the past 10 years he was secretary of the organisation.

Mr Cleland was president of the recently formed Totara Valley Tennis Club, being one of the prime movers in its formation and taking a keen interest in the laying down of the courts. Mr Cleland's father was one of the foundation members and office bearers of the local Presbyterian church, in this connection his son, Andrew was a worthy successor of a worthy parent. In everything pertaining to the welfare of this Church he took an active interest. In May 1921 he was elected to the position of elder and served faithfully in that office till he was called to higher service.

Mr Cleland is survived by his widow and nine children. The interment took place at the Pleasant Point Cemetery the funeral being one of the largest seen there. At the graveside the Rev. W. NcNeur made feeling reference to the good life that had been lived. A special in memoriam service was held in St Pauls Church, Totara Valley.

Obituary in the Outlook

Through the death of Mr A. J. Cleland the charge of Pleasant Point has lost one of its leading members. Brought up in the district, Mr Cleland was all his life connected with the Totara Valley congregation, in which he was ordained to the office of elder in May 1921. Besides being a churchman Mr Cleland was ever active in seeking to promote the welfare of the whole community, and by his kindly unselfish nature he endeared himself to everyone. A special In Memoriam Service was held in St Paul's Church Totara Valley when the Rev W. McNeur spoke on the text "Our

Saviour Jesus Christ hath abolished death and hath brought life and immortality to light through the Gospel" II Tim. 1:10.

Much sympathy is felt for the relatives in their time of sorrow. Mr Cleland's life though comparatively short was rich in good works.

Wordsworth has said "That best portion of a good man's life. His little, nameless, unremembered acts of kindness and of love".

And we thank God for a life so well lived in the service of the Master.

Now it is time for me to share my memories of Dad. I was very fond of him and held him in great respect. Dad was a gentle, peace-loving man with a kind generous heart. Although he was very good to us, he did discipline us when we needed it. He had a sense of humour and often enjoyed a joke. I can remember Dad being very thoughtful and generous to our next-door neighbours, the Histen Family who brought up another family as well as their own under very difficult circumstances.

When I was small, he called me Tuppence, so Jessie started to call me Tup and even to this day Olive often calls me by that name. Later as I grew older, Dad called me Mrs Polish because on a Saturday morning, my job was to clean all the shoes and boots other members of the family had thrown in the bottom of the cylinder cupboard to dry.

Dad was a good public speaker and our family was always proud of him when he was in leadership at public functions. I can remember the enthusiasm he showed when it was decided to build tennis courts at Totara Valley and how he loved a game of tennis and encouraged us to play.

As Dad's parents died before I was born, I don't remember them. However, I did receive a legacy of £135 from my grandmother Margaret Cleland's estate in 1953.

Dad's brothers and especially his sisters were very gentle people. I have lovely memories of Aunty Jean who taught me at Sunday

School and of our blind Aunty Madge who sometimes stayed in our home. Her wonderful faith had an effect on my life.

We knew Uncle Robert and his family very well because they lived down the road at Loudoun, where our Cleland grandparents had brought up their family. What a shock it was to our family when our Aunty Olive died suddenly in 1927 at the age of 33 years. Over the years, we saw how the loss of their mother affected our cousins.

The Shepherd Family

Now a little about Mum's side of the family. James Shepherd, Mum's father had the misfortune to lose his wife when Mum was five years old. He married again, so I only remember my step-grandmother who had no family of her own. Granddad Shepherd farmed at Sutherlands, but I only remember him living in Timaru on the eastern corner of Church and Preston Street. The old home is still there. I have recollections of Jessie and me staying with them, not very happy times.

Granddad was a keen bowler and I can remember going to the Westend Bowling green with him and watching him play. He was always good to us, but I heard from others that he had a very quick temper and could be very unforgiving. By the time I knew him, he had lost his four sons (two as babies) and only had his two daughters, Mum and my Aunty Nell.

The following is a copy of his life written in an encyclopaedia:

> James Shepherd who was born in Forfarshire Scotland on 2nd November 1842 emigrated to Queensland in 1866. Later moved to Southland for two years and then to Otago for five years. In 1873 came to South Canterbury, where he started contract ploughing in the Cave area. He ploughed some of the Burnett estate from tussock. There was a paddock on Jim Kelynack's farm at Cannington called Shepherd's paddock where he had camped with his horses.
>
> In 1881 he bought 400 acres from the New Zealand and Australian Land Company at Sutherlands. He named the place Dunnichen Farm which had a fine view of the plains to the sea from the house. He planted a plantation of pine and gum trees for shelter. He cropped areas for grain and also had a flock of Leicester sheep.

18

For several years he served on the Sutherlands school committee being chairman for a time. He also took an interest in the St Paul's Presbyterian Church at Pleasant Point, services being held in the Sutherlands School once a month.

He retired to Timaru where he enjoyed a past time of Bowls, being an early member of the Westend men's bowling club.

Granddad Shepherd did have foresight, because he left each member of our family money to receive when aged 25 years, but he included a clause that we could receive it earlier if we needed it for education.

I received the following amounts from his estate.

Advances for School Board	1.03.38	£15/10
	5.07.38	£15/10
	11.10.38	£15/10
Wedding	10.10.45	£53/10
First Payment	13.02.46	£118/15/9
(£230 less advances)		
Second Payment		
(in 3 percent Govt Stock)	10.09.52	£525
Final Payment	10.09.52	£191/13/13

Tough Times

Now I will return to our family situation after Dad died. Mum was left in a poor financial situation with money owed to a stock firm. Our Uncle Robert and Uncle Jim were trustees of Dad's estate, so Uncle Robert decided what was to be done on the farm. My brother Les was already on the farm with Dad, but he didn't see eye-to-eye with Uncle Robert, so it wasn't long before he left home. From then on, we had so many different men working on the farm, you could write a book on them.

With the loss of Dad and financial difficulties, Mum became anxious and worried, and often very confused. She was very difficult to live with at times. She worked very hard, but at times went to extremes, like rising at 4.30 am on a Monday to do the washing.

Mum was very proud of the butter she made and she sold it to the staff of the CFCA grocery department to get some cash.

Education

At this time Mum was thoughtful for us and used the interest that she received from the money Granddad Shepherd had left her to pay for Lloyd (and later Jim) to board at Boys High School. They received an education. She also paid my bus fare to attend the Point School from that interest.

Mum did have compassion, because she was always happy to care for anyone who was sick. Several times I remember her looking after our cousin Willie White's wife, who had been an English war bride and had ill health. Our home was always open for our school friends. I can remember Lloyd and Jim bringing friends home from boarding school for weekends. I know I was free to have friends to stay.

Looking back to my secondary school days at the Point District High School, I am thankful for the education I received. I had great admiration for our two teachers, Mr Easterbrook and Miss McBean. They taught every subject to all the classes from Form III to Form 6, whether it was their specialist subject or not. They were also responsible for coaching us in our sports activities. Miss McBean was an excellent basketball coach and our A team did well in matches against other District High School teams.

During the years I was going to the Point School, my sister Jessie and I grew together in a very close companionship, as we shared all our joys and problems. Jessie had to leave school in her fourth form year because she developed colitis, a terrible embarrassing disease. She had been boarding at Grandma Shepherds with Margaret and attending Girls High School. I felt so sorry for her because the doctors didn't have a cure. It was years later before she had an improvement in her health.

Timaru Girls High School

After I passed my matriculation at Point School, Mum decided I should attend Timaru Girls High in my sixth form year. During that year 1938, I boarded privately with Mrs Lyne who lived at 46

Victoria Street. Some of the money that Granddad Shepherd had left me was used to pay for the board.

Mrs Lyne was a special landlady and her daughter Lily, who was engaged to be married to Roly Bracefield, was very good to me. Jean Gudsell (later Dellow) shared a room with me. Changing schools was a big challenge. I did miss home, especially Jessie, and I was very homesick for the first three weeks. Regarding school work, I found I was just as far ahead in my subjects as the other girls in my class. I benefitted from greater competition and a change of principals.

I had no way of going home for weekends, so I appreciated Margaret coming in from Pareora, where she was teaching, to spend Saturday with me. We often went shopping and she often bought things for me that I would never have had otherwise.

On Sundays, I often went with Jim, who was boarding at Thomas House, to Grandma Shepherd's for the day after we had been to church. Sometimes Bessie invited us to the home of her mother Mrs Beck for dinner.

That year saw the first marriages in our family. Les and Bessie were married on 31 August and Sadie and Viv were married on 21 December.

Teachers College

Before the end of the school year, with others in my class, I applied for teachers College and we were accepted to attend Christchurch College in 1939. We applied for board at one of the hostels and were accepted. During the year I had formed a friendship with Joyce Buckley and we planned to share a room at the hostel. Much to our disappointment, during the school holidays, all the South Canterbury entrants for College received word that we were transferred to Dunedin College. This meant we had to accept private board because the hostels in Dunedin were already fully booked.

Joyce and I boarded with a Mrs Alexander, a widow at 26 Duke Street. She also boarded her niece Aggie Stewart, who attended Otago Girls High School, another relative June Duthie, a training college student and Frances Mottram, later Forster, the mother of Dr Forster in Timaru. Frances was doing research at the University. Mrs Alexander was a very keen bowler, but she didn't provide very good board or meals. We paid 25 shillings a week board out of our salary of 100 pounds a year

We walked to the College, which was conducted in a three-story building on Union Street, but at the beginning of the third term, we shifted into a new two-story building, further down Union Street opposite Logan Park. I enjoyed my time at Training College, spending one month having lectures and the next month on section in a school with a teacher and class. We had to take "Crit" lessons to be judged by the teacher or by a lecturer from the College.

During the first year in Dunedin, we experienced the worst snowfall that the city had ever had. Mrs Alexander's home was surrounded by eighteen inches or more of snow. The College and the schools were closed for four days.

Another milestone that year was the beginning of World War 2. At the end of the August holidays, Joyce and I were returning to Dunedin on the midnight train and I can remember hearing on arriving in Dunedin that war had been declared. The war didn't affect the majority of the male students, because they were too young to go to war, but I can remember the whole College going to the railway station to farewell Errol Allison, a student who was old enough to go.

A long and lasting friendship with Sheila Diehl commenced for me that first year at College. We were both in the same mixed section. Sheila and I always went to church together, because Joyce Buckley attended the Anglican Church. Sheila and I spent many happy times together staying in each other's homes during our holidays. I got to know her family very well.

In December of 1939, I had the pleasure of being bridesmaid for my sister Margaret when she and Evan Chapman were married at Pleasant Point. I always loved my frock, which was made of pink georgette.

Before the end of 1939, Joyce and I arranged different board for the next year up on the hill at 3 Dundas St. Our new landlady, Mrs McNamara provided board for twelve College students with the help of her daughter Frances. What a difference! We were given beautiful meals in a dining room of our own and were never allowed inside the kitchen. Warm hotties were put in our beds each night.

By this time, Joyce was engaged to Cliff Bissett, who had gone overseas in the army. Later in 1940, Joyce shifted to live with Cliff's mother who lived in Dunedin. Marion Stobo, a college student from Southland, roomed with me. Joyce's relationship came to a sad end. Their marriage was arranged for when Cliff returned home, but when he arrived, he told Joyce he had met someone else overseas and broke off their engagement. It was a terrible disappointment for her, but later on in her life, she married Ray Grant and they lived in Dunedin.

Teacher at Point

The two years at Training College passed quickly and I was pleased to be given the position of probationary assistant at the Pleasant Point District High School for 1941. That year I travelled daily to school on the school bus that passed our home. I enjoyed the class of primer 3 and 4 children that I taught. Miss Price was the Infant Mistress and taught Primers 1 and 2. She was an excellent teacher and I learnt far more from her than I had during my College Days.

The next year after I had taught a month at the Point School, the Education Board asked me to relieve for a time at the sole charge School in Cannington. I was very disappointed at this change of plan, but I didn't realise how it was going to affect my life by bringing Rod and me together. To get to Cannington, I had to travel by bus to Timaru and then catch another bus that travelled through Cannington to Fairlie. I was told by the Chairman of the Cannington School Committee to get off at McKenzie's place where I would be given board. Rod's Mother and Helen made me most welcome. Later I discovered that Rod didn't want his mother to board me because I was a woman school teacher.

Cannington

Teaching at Cannington was very different, as I had to teach all classes, from the infants to Form II. I had to be well organized for everything to run smoothly. I found the pupils a lovely group of children, especially the senior ones, Frank and Martin Casey. They were so helpful and did endeavour to do their work well. What I did miss was the company of the other teachers at Point. Each day I walked to school and was able to work after school to make preparations for the next day. Because of travelling difficulties, I had to stay weekends at Cannington. On Sundays, I went to Church with the McKenzie Family and got to know many people in the district.

My time at Cannington turned out to be longer than had I expected, because a soldier who was overseas was appointed to the position and it had to be re-advertised as an indirect war appointment. This resulted in me experiencing my first winter in the Cannington district. The school was a cold place with only a fire place to heat it.

As time went on, Rod and I became friends. In July, I applied for the position at the Cannington School as well as for one at the Pleasant Point School. I was pleased to be appointed to the one at the Point School. As a result, I left Cannington at the end of the second term in August, having formed a better opinion of the district than I had when I was sent there.

Pleasant Point Again

When I started the new position at the Point School, I taught Standard 3 and 4, a good class. Instead of living at home, Miss Price the infant mistress asked me to live with her in the house she rented. This was a real blessing for me. I was able to go home at the weekends. Miss Price was a lovely lady and she and I related well to each other. She loved to spend time in the garden, while I prepared and cooked our evening meal.

In the following year 1943, I taught Standard 1 and 2, which was another good class, and I continued to live with Miss Price. During February, Rod and I were engaged. Every second weekend, Rod would ride his horse or his bike over to Newburgh and stay Saturday night with us. On the in-between weekends, we had to be content with writing letters. We didn't have any social life together, because there was petrol rationing for the war. Occasionally we were able to go together to a function at Cave, when soldiers were being farewelled.

In 1943 we had a change of headmaster at the Point School. Mr Gibb left and was replaced by Mr McRae, who didn't stay long. It was during his time at Point that Miss Price asked if I could teach Primer 3 and 4 instead of her, so that she did not have a different first-year teacher every year in the Infant Department. That really suited me, because I enjoyed teaching that age group. I taught with Miss Price until I resigned from teaching.

I sometimes went with Miss Price when we were invited out for meals. It was with her that I attended my first Bible Study Group led by the Rev. Ian Dixon. At this time, I started teaching Sunday

School at Totara Valley. Unfortunately, the Rev Dixon was called into the army, so the Bible Study Group and the Good Companions Group which he had started for the Youth closed down.

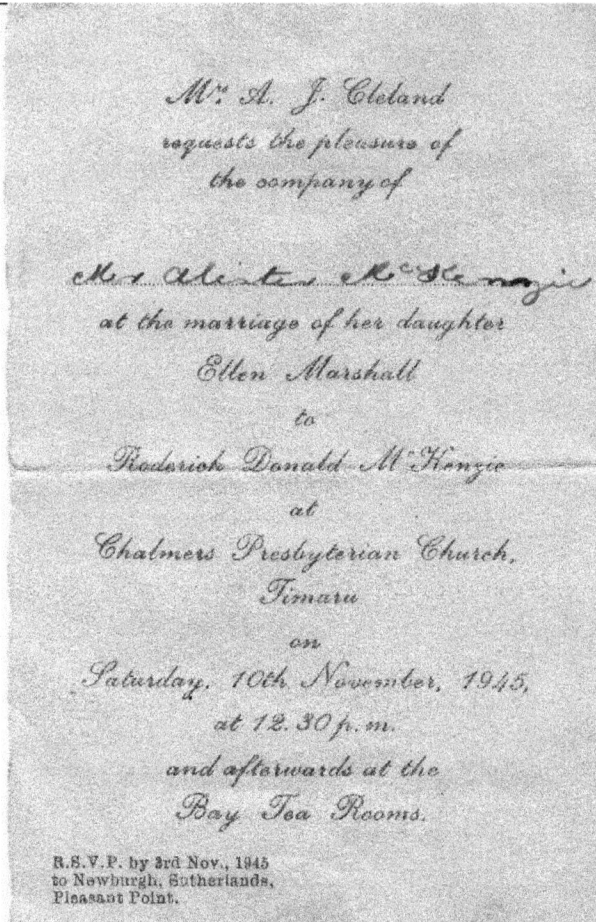

Mr A. J. Cleland
requests the pleasure of
the company of

Mrs Alister McKenzie
at the marriage of her daughter
Ellen Marshall
to
Roderick Donald McKenzie
at
Chalmers Presbyterian Church,
Timaru
on
Saturday, 10th November, 1945,
at 12.30 p.m.
and afterwards at the
Bay Tea Rooms.

R.S.V.P. by 3rd Nov., 1945
to Newburgh, Sutherlands,
Pleasant Point.

Several events happened during my last year of teaching in 1945. Firstly, in February there was a big flood which flooded parts of Pleasant Point. Both approaches to the Opihi Bridge were washed out, leaving a busload of sightseers stranded on the bridge overnight – a frightening experience for them. The school was closed for several days. Then in July, a storm brought nine inches of snow which disrupted communication. The school was closed for four days.

At this time, I was living at home, because Jessie was in the Mater Hospital in Dunedin Hospital for six months. She was under the care of Dr Everach for her colitis problem. During the time Jessie was in Dunedin, I stayed with Mum and helped her to milk the cows, before I caught the school bus in the mornings.

This was a difficult time. A great blessing was that some time earlier, Aunty Nell had come to live with and care for Grandma Shepherd. She was always so understanding and we could always share our problems with her.

At the end of September, I resigned from my position at the Point School. October was spent making final preparations for our wedding and doing up the entire garden before Jessie returned home at the beginning of November.

Wedding

Preparing for our wedding and buying clothes wasn't easy, because we had clothing coupons to limit what we bought. My sister Peg helped us out, because people with children didn't use all their coupons. Even the material for my wedding frock had to be bought with coupons.

The great day, November 10th eventually came. Rod and I were married in Chalmers Church at 12.30 p.m. by the Rev Norman Oakley. Following the service, we had the reception in the Caroline Bay Tearooms. In those days we had an afternoon tea with sweets, followed by sandwiches and cakes.

A norwester blew through the night, before the weather changed to the south, but it didn't rain. Aunty Nell was delighted for us to use Grandma's home to get dressed for the wedding. Rod and I also changed there after the wedding, before Evan Chapman drove us out to Temuka to catch the train to Christchurch. Although the war had ended, petrol was still being rationed. We spent most of our honeymoon at Akaroa, depending on buses for transport.

On arriving home, we found that the Saunders hadn't shifted out of the Parira house, so we had to stay two weeks with Rod's mother. I was delighted when we finally got settled in our home. There was plenty to do, as the garden was neglected. During the Christmas holidays, we had many visitors, including Jessie, Mary, Olive and Sheila. While Sheila was with us, she and I made our first attempt at wallpapering. Our workmanship was far from perfect, but what a difference it made to the lounge and our bedroom. We were very pleased with our efforts.

Buying a Farm
(Rod)

Len Saunders

Len Saunders had offered to lease his farm to me, but nothing came of it. However, one day when I came back from mustering at Nimrod, Uncle Jack said Len would sell the farm for £10 an acre. Uncle Jack would go around the sheep for me while Alan was at war and Alister was in camp. He had been talking to Len and he said he was keen to sell the farm. Uncle Jack said I should go and make an offer.

I had saved up the deposit for a farm, but I knew it would be very hard to get one, as all available land was being bought for returned servicemen. Every sale had to go through the Land Court and if it was suitable for returned servicemen, the sale could be cancelled. I used to study the paper each Saturday to find suitable land. I thought I might have to move up to Northland, where there seemed to be good opportunities, but I knew they were probably not as good as they sounded.

Len Saunders' farm was so run down it had been turned down for returned servicemen, being classed as uneconomic. He had worked very hard, but was no farmer. He did not know how to farm on hills and he was useless with horses. They had brought some heifer calves down from Methven with them and had built up a herd of 30 cows, but the cows used all of the best land, so the sheep suffered. Mrs Saunders worked very hard milking cows. She also grew raspberries and eggs to sell. Len got into trouble with the National Mortgage Agency and started growing wheat to earn some cash. He had taken three crops of wheat in a row off the long ridge.

When Mr Saunders knew I was interested in the farm, his price went up to £13-10 an acre, the price that he had paid ten years earlier. I managed to knock him down to £12-5 an acre. He never told me that the farm did not belong to him.

The sale had to go through the Land Court. Len came to me one day and said that if the sale did not go through the court by the next Friday, the sale would be cancelled. I still thought he wanted to sell it to me, but he had actually had an offer at £13-10 from an agent wanting it for returned servicemen. The returned servicemen could buy it at 1942 prices and the government would make up the difference.

I became very worried. I had told Mr Howell from Nimrod that I was buying the farm and he had encouraged me, so I spoke with him. Mr Howell was a friend of Mr Robertson who was the Chairman of the Land Court in Timaru, so he phoned him. Mr Robertson said for us to meet him at the Grosvenor Hotel the next day at 10 a.m.

Mr Howell drove me to Timaru in his car. He parked the car and we walked to the hotel. When we got to Beswick Street, he J-walked across the intersection. When we got to the other side, a policeman told us off. Mr Howell was deaf, so he did not hear what the policeman was saying. I was really embarrassed, but I could not say anything, so I just pretended that I did not hear.

Mr Robertson listened to what I had to say and Mr Howell put in a good word for me. Mr Robertson then said he would see what he could do. That night Mr Saunders got a phone call to say the sale had been approved by the Land Court. He called me and said that the farm was mine.

Mr Greenslade

I helped Mr Saunders arrange the clearing sale. Mr Greenslade, a cousin of Mr Saunders, came to the sale with his son. I had thought he was a good man and got on well with him. He was very strong and worked hard. He always came down to help at shearing and when lambs were being sold and stayed till all the work was done. I thought he was being kind, because Mr Saunders needed the help.

I did not buy much at the clearing sale, because everything was such poor quality. Afterwards, the auctioneer came and asked if I would buy some sheep that had not sold. I knew the age of some four-tooth ewes, which had poor mouths, because they had been grazed too hard. I bought them, because I knew they would be good, and turned them out onto the Cliff Paddock.

That night Mr Greenslade called at Riverbank and asked why I had been buying sheep. I told him that I had bought the farm from Len. He said that the farm was not Len's to sell. Len had just been managing it, because he had bought it in Lens name. I did not argue. I just explained that I had paid for the farm and that the title had been transferred by a solicitor and the Land Court had approved. He then realised that there was not much that he could do, so he left.

I had worked with Len for many years, but it had never occurred to me that he was in financial trouble. It seemed that Len Saunders had gradually come to think that the farm was his own. Mr Greenslade did not know the farm had been sold and had come down to buy the stock at the auction to farm it himself. He had bought a few sheep, when his son Willard noticed that I was buying. He told his father to be careful, so he stopped buying stock.

When Ellen and I got back from our honeymoon, we were surprised to find that Mr Saunders was still there. Mr Greenslade had taken the money I paid for the farm, so Len had not been able to buy a place to take his cows. He asked if he could lease some land for them, until he found a place to go. I agreed that he could for a while, but I said that I wanted the house.

The Saunders sent their children to relatives and moved into the old hut by the garage. I bought the coal range down from Greenridge and put it in the hut for them. They eventually left in March, when he got some land to graze his cows on. The last of

Len Saunders livestock and equipment were loaded onto a truck on 24 May 1946.

Later when Margaret was teaching at Ruapuna, I discovered the full story. Mr Greenslade had leased a farm at Shepherd's Bush. He owed money to the owner of the farm and they had a fight in which Mr Greenslade was hit on the head with a standard. One night, the stock and plant that Mr Greenslade owned just disappeared. He had taken it down to Cannington to the farm there. He had bought the farm in his cousin's name, so the man he owed the money could not get at it.

I called the farm Parira, which means Sun on the Cliffs. Uncle Jack got this translated into Maori for me. I had spent all my life looking up at these cliffs with the sun shining on them.

> Took possession of farm from Len Saunders on 17/10/45 and called it "Parira". Ellen and I took possession of the house on 20/12/45 and I trust that with God's help, we will spend many happy years at Parira (Diary 1/1/46).

Financing the Farm

When I bought the farm in 1945, I had saved £1400. I paid a deposit of £700 and gave Ellen £200 to buy some furniture. At the clearing sale, I bought the wool press and shearing plant and a few sheep.

I took over the existing mortgages on the farm. The first mortgage was with Government Life. There was also a second mortgage with Mr Gainsford for £800. I paid it off quite quickly, as these were good years for farming. The mortgage with Government Life was good, because it rolled over every five years. The interest was fixed at 5% and never changed. The Government Life was pleased to get a better farmer onto the property, as Len Saunders had been having trouble paying the interest.

This mortgage had originally been held by Ellen's aunts. In his early days, Mr Gainsford was struggling on the farm. He approached Mr Shepherd for advice, as he was reputed to be a good farmer. Mr Shepherd brought Mr Cleland over with him and they looked over the farm together. They lent him money, and the mortgage was still there when Len Saunders bought the farm. He must have changed it to the Government Life.

Robins Farm

The farm next door to Parira was first owned by Mr Gainsford's brother. Other owners were Chris Cooper and Jim Calder. None of these men had been successful farmers. When I bought Parira, the farm was owned by Mr Robins.

I wanted to buy the farm and had meant to approach Mr Robins about it. I met his son Eric on the road one day and he said his father was sick and wanted to sell. I told him that I was interested and suggested that he should come and see me. Mr Robins eventually came up and I offered £18 an acre, but he wanted £23. We eventually agreed on £20 and signed the deal on 17 April 1953.

Joe Scott took an objection to the Land Court. Mr Robins disliked Catholics, so he did not want Mr Scott to get the farm. His first wife was a Catholic and the priest had put a lot of pressure on him to bring his children up as Catholics. He told me that if the Land Court turned down the sale, he would withdraw it from the market, and lease it to me. The court action failed. Mr Scott rung up to tell me, and he did not seem to bear any ill will.

Mr Robins wanted me to have the farm, because I had given him a lot of help. He had done quite a lot of dealing in stock. One year he bought some Hereford heifers. They spent most of their time on my farm, by pushing through the gorse fence into the Windmill Paddock. I think that they liked the grass there better, because I had been putting on lime. I was glad when they were sold.

I took possession of Mr Robin's farm at the end of May. I shifted the plough and the tractor down to the new farm and started ploughing almost straight away. Having Robin's farm really gave me a very economic unit. The access to Parira was improved significantly because the gully in Eric's Paddock was good for coming down with a loaded dray or wagon. If you got out of control, you could veer either way and go uphill.

Robin's farm needed a lot of development. The Swamp Paddock was a problem, as the swamp was gradually creeping out into the paddock. In 1954 when a dragline was in the district, I got it to come and put in a drain along the bottom of the cliff. This got rid of the swamp. There was a spring at the top and the drain always had a continuous trickle of water. I also got a bulldozer in to widen the cutting up behind the Robin's house to improve the access up on to the hills.

Cooper's Flat was another problem, as most of the time, it was swampy and difficult to access. A man from the Department of Agriculture came and put a ditch along the bottom of the back facing in 1955. It drained out onto the cliff at the bottom end of the flat. He measured all the levels and had a special plough. This made a tremendous difference to Coopers Flat. There was a big spring at the top of the flat, so I put a drain into the creek. I now had a really good paddock, and in a dry year, it would carry a lot of stock.

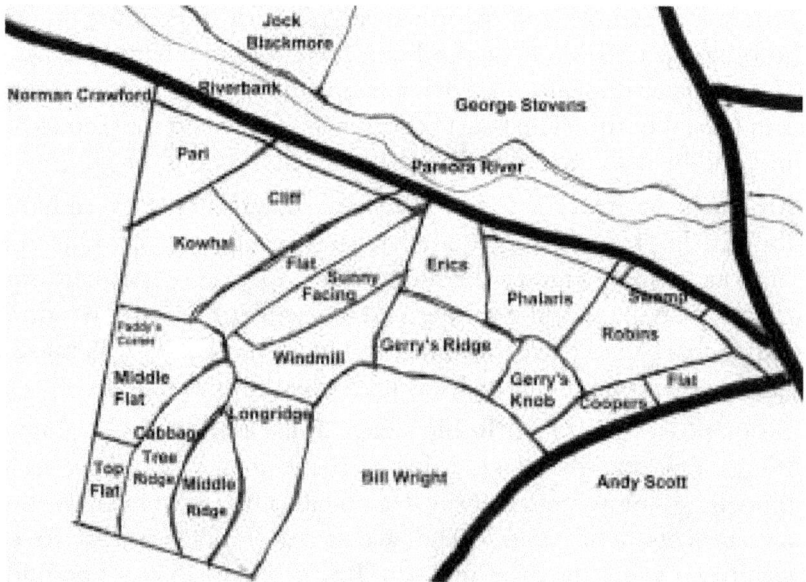

Developing Parira

First Year (from Rod's Diary)

The impression from his 1946 diary is that Rod did a lot of work to remedy the damage done by Mr Saunder's cropping and cows. A lot of the fences needed to be repaired. He borrowed a scoop from Mr Lamb and cleaned out the dams. Much time was taken up with ploughing. The following paddocks were cultivated that year: Top Flat, Cabbage Tree Ridge, Middle Ridge, and Long Ridge. The Windmill Paddock and the Flat had already been cultivated. In the next two years, he also ploughed the Pari Paddock, Cliff Paddock, Middle Flat and Kowhai Paddock. He planted oats, turnips, swedes, rape, Italian and H1 ryegrass.

Rod and Alister worked closely together to keep the team working. One would look round the sheep for the other, if he was busy. During the winter, Rod spent several evenings working with a new horse for Alister. A month later he noted that it was going well. The next day he took him for a ride around the block.

A lot of farming equipment was borrowed from other people: Jim Calder's tractor and trailer, a horse from Norman Crawford, a scoop from Mr Lamb, rams from Mr Crawford and Mr Howell, a topdresser from Uncle Bob Wisely, a roller from the Crawfords, harrows from Jim Calder, a handpiece from Mr Howell (shearers did not own their own in those days, but used those supplied by the farmer). Rod also helped a number of other farmers with their work, dipping sheep for Jim Calder, shoeing horses for Jack Martin and Mr Gillingham, harvesting for Campbells, mustering Smith's Block for the Howells, stacking for Uncle Bob.

In March, Rod went to the Holme Station ewe fair and bought 70 of Ford's ewes for 17/9. Jack Martin drove them home for Rod. He would have been bringing other sheep into the district. The sale was not as good as the Point ewe fair.

Uncle Jack provided a lot of help. He went around the sheep when Alister and Rod were busy. In March he brought down a meat safe that he had built for Ellen.

Rod and Ellen with Alan

The first lambing was quite a difficult one. Rain came on 24, 25 and 29 September and snow on 1 October, but the lamb losses were not great. Rod tailed about 446 lambs, including 80 sets of twins.

Clipping the horses took about three days in May. In the winter Rod spent several days making ropes from twine and working at the forge fixing chains and making hooks. A few days would be spent repairing harness and saddles.

Expenditure for January 1946

Government Life Insurance	£63/12/11
H Squire baling	£11
Cave Stores	£6/10/10
CFCA Radio	£17/18/6
CFCA Furniture	£79/19/4
A Curtis pup	£5
Cave Store	£5/1/10
CFCA seeds	£3/10/0
Dalgetys Coal	£2/6/6
D Unwin Meatsafe Wardrobe	£8/5/0
Cave Store	£3/5/6
SC Electric Power Board	£7/2/0
NMA sheep dip, wool packs	£4/3/0
NM Insurance	£1/13/9

Twitch and Thistles (Rod)

When I took over Parira, it was cropped out. It had been a good farm, but Mr Saunders had got into financial trouble and had grown three crops of wheat in a row on the best parts of the farm to get some cash. The Long Ridge was full of Californian thistles and twitch. The Cliff Paddock was the same and was pugged up by cows as well.

I would hang around with the farmers after church to see what I could learn. One day Fred Rapley said, "I know how to get rid of twitch". He said to plough it and when it comes up green to plough it again. If this was repeated several times, the twitch would die. This worked for me. I shallow ploughed the Long Ridge first. It was so hard for the horses to push through the thistles, that I hung sacks on their harness to protect them. The second time I deep ploughed the paddock. The third time I ploughed it with a disc plough I borrowed from Jim Calder. All the thistles and twitch soon turned to humus and the soil was lovely and fertile. I sowed it in H1 ryegrass, which was new, and got an enormous crop of grass. I also ploughed the Cliff Paddock.

I used a hillside disk plough on the Kowhai Paddock. I bought it cheap at a clearing sale. It could go in both directions, so you just had to turn the horses around at the edge of the paddock. It was still up on the back facing of the Kowhai Paddock when I left the farm.

Whenever we ploughed a paddock, thousands of seagulls would turn up to grab the fresh worms and other bugs from the fresh soil. They would dive in right at the back of the plough as the furrow turned. Sometimes they would bomb the ploughman with a white splodge.

Lime

The whole farm was very hungry, so I put on a lot of lime. Ellen bought the first 40 ton with part of her inheritance from Granddad Shepherd. It came from Oamaru, free by rail. Mr Hawthorne, who owned the Cave Transport, carried 20 ton over and placed the bags around the Cliff Paddock. I spread it with a lime box pulled by horses. The bags weighed 1.5 hundredweight so they were heavy to handle. My diary says, "The first lime to be sown on Parira was a gift from my wife". Mr Hawthorne carted the remaining twenty ton of lime into the woolshed. A week later, I borrowed Jim Calder's tractor and trailer and spent two days spreading the rest of the lime on the sunny facing of the Windmill Paddock

I put the lime on the grass paddocks. It made such a difference you could see the pieces that I missed. Mr Baker had used a lot of lime and Mr Darling was pushing it too. Norman spread a lot of lime at the same time, as he had worked for the Bakers and seen what a difference it made. The Department of Agriculture advised us to start putting on a ton to the acre. We had been putting on about a hundredweight per acre, but that was not enough.

In 1949, St Andrew's Transport spread lime on the Middle and Cabbage Tree Ridges and the Lucerne Paddock. Getting a contractor was a much easier way to spread it.

Spreading a ton of lime to the acre in a paddock before it was sowed down in pasture soon became the normal practice. The transport companies all bought bulk spreaders for this purpose. The lime transformed farming in Cannington. At last, we were able to grow good pasture.

The Railway Goods Shed

Mr Fitzgerald was a railway worker during the day. He must have been paid a little extra to be caretaker at night, so when we had to go over at night to pick up stuff from the goods shed, we would have to get the key from him. He was very officious and difficult to deal with. Once when the freezing works sent back the carcasses of some lambs that had been rejected, I remember pleading with him for the key. I think that he was reluctant to give it out, because some farmers took advantage of the goods shed. One had put his wheat in the shed and then refused to shift it.

One time I got 40 ton of lime from Oamaru. Mr Fitzgerald would not let me leave it in the wagons and he would not let me put it in the goods shed. I had to get the Cave Transport to carry it over and put it in our woolshed. It nearly sank into the ground under the weight. I borrowed Jim Calder's crawler tractor and carried it out into the paddocks and then spread it with the horses and the spreader.

There was such a demand for lime that a limeworks was opened just down the road from Cave. The lime was carried over the river in a bucket on a cable and then crushed on our side of the river.

Sheep

I always fed my sheep well. I learned when I was shearing that farms with heavy sheep got more wool. Those with light skinny sheep tended to have poor wool and no money. I resolved back then that I would always have good well-fed stock.

From my shearing, I knew who had good sheep. For the first few years, I bought sheep from the Howell's. They were cheap and had good mouths, but gave trouble with foot rot. However, they were very good milkers.

The second year I brought sheep from Phil Green at Straven. They were a mixture of four and five-year-old ewes and were really rough, but they were cheap. I had to sneak them home so people would not see them and laugh at me.

Early on, I started buying ewes from the McPhersons. They were Lincoln/Merino/Half-bred cross. They were good milkers, and they shifted down onto our farm really well. Being genuine four-year olds, I was getting them at their best. I kept them for three years and would get at least three lambs from them. I would then sell them as one-year ewes and get a good price. I continued to buy McPherson's sheep until Hamish started going back into Romneys. (I knew what would happen to them.)

I learned early on that it was important to have sheep that milked well. Parira really suited early fat lambs, as it got very dry later in the summer. I always wanted good milking ewes, so that I could get as many lambs as possible away to the freezing works off their mothers. This enabled me to cope with the dry summer. I also found that good milkers have a lot of twins.

The Romney breeders were concentrating on breeding a sheep with a Southdown body and wool all over. The original Romney had been open-faced. Alister called Romneys "milkless wonders". He got to the stage where he could not get a fat lamb away from his Romneys. They were very highly regarded in Cannington, but many people were finding it difficult to produce fat lambs.

The sheep Mum had on Riverbank were great milkers. Dad had been buying hill ewes at Albury and Fairlie ewe fairs and using Border Leister rams. After he died, Uncle Bob told Mum that she would not do well with old ewes. He talked her into keeping some ewe lambs for breeding stock. I had helped her pick out some good ones with open faces. They proved to be great producers and I always looked back to that.

At that time, a lot of people were using Border Corriedales. I thought, "Why not do the same with Romneys". Some people were using the Border Leisters as a fat lamb sire to get extra weight. I bought my first Border Romney cross ewe lambs from Jim Little who had been doing this. Eric Feather told me I was making a mistake and that I would get all single lambs. He was wrong, and I found that big sheep have lots of twins.

I got the fat lamb drafters to look for good sized Border Romney cross lambs. I would pay a shilling more than fat price for the big ewe lambs, so drafters would run off the best ewe lambs for me. Ian Woolford bought a lot of good ewe lambs for me this way.

I later heard Professor Coop speak at a field day at Bakers. He was experimenting with what would later be called Coopworth. I had already been doing the same thing for a number of years, but I had kept what I was doing secret. I did not even tell Jim Campbell, as he would think that I had lost my mind.

Some people said that because Border Romney cross sheep had bare faces and bare legs, they would not produce much wool. This was not true. The first year I had Border Romney cross ewes, my wool weights increased significantly. The only weakness with the Border Romney cross was that they were susceptible to footrot. Romneys did cope better because they came from the English marshes.

I bought Border Leister rams and bred them with Romney ewes. I always preferred the first cross to get the benefits of hybrid vigour. Later I started buying Coopworth rams from the Darlings. They always sorted out good producers for me. Alister focused on Coopworths from the beginning. His Romney ewes had got so poor that he was getting less than 100 percent lambing percentage.

Tussle with Norman

I always bought McPherson's ewes at the ewe fair, as we found this a good way to establish a fair price. In 1952, Norman Crawford told me that he was going to bid against me. He had seen over the fence that McPherson's ewes were good producers. My other neighbours were shocked, as this was something you did not do, but Norman was thick-skinned and did not worry about what they thought. The night before the sale, I spoke to Sandy McPherson and got him to agree that if I bought them at auction this year, he would sell them to me on the place next year. At the auction, the whole district was watching to see what would happen. Henry

41

Campbell said, "I will stand beside you and tell you what Norman is doing".

I just kept bidding until I had the winning bid of 66/-, three times what I had paid for ewes a few years earlier. That night Sandy McPherson phoned and said, "I hear you paid a big price for the ewes". He had not been at the sale. When I agreed, he said, "Come up here tomorrow. There are another twenty-eight ewes here you can have in exchange for a few bales of Lucerne hay." Norman never knew that I got those extra sheep, and next year I bought them on the place without going to the auction. I got 138 at 65/- and 59 for £2.

Ill Thrift

Ill thrift was a serious problem for lambs. It arrived in about 1938 and there was nothing much that could be done, as there were no good drenches. In the late 1950s, I experimented with Brown Trotter's drench. He was looked upon as a crank, but his drench made up of a mixture of copper sulphate (bluestone) sulphate of iron and cobalt seemed to work. I saw the difference when I drenched some lambs before sending them down to rape at St Andrews. Another man was grazing his lambs on the same rape. All over South Canterbury lambs were failing to thrive on rape. Mine all went away fat, but the other man's did poorly.

I had a ewe in the Cow Paddock with twins and they were doing poorly. As an experiment, I gave one a dose of the drench. In a few weeks, it was hard to believe they were twins, as one had done so well.

I did not get the same results in later years, but by then I had started putting on trace elements with superphosphate and this seemed to deal with the problem. In later years, better drenches like Thiabenzole dealt with parasites better.

Cattle

I bought my first cattle from Hedley Squire. They were 10 Devon/Shorthorn cross heifers. They really did well, so I would go up there every year in the spring and buy some cattle. He would have them all in pens with each pen priced. We never argued about the price, as I would always pay what he asked.

His farm was always cold in the spring and the cattle often looked awful, so I got them quite cheap. I was really embarrassed driving them down the road and often hoped Henry Campbell would not be in his yards and see them go by. They did really well on Parira, and Hedley often used me for advertising. When I was selling them at the Point sale, he would often have some clients there to see them. Sometimes he would put a few bids in to help the price along.

The YFC had a fat cattle competition in those days and I would quite often win. One of the judges was Marty Wilson, who bought a lot of cattle for the butchers in Timaru. He would look out for my cattle at the sale and buy them.

> In the 1950 YFC fat cattle competition, I got first and second in the over-two year. Later that year I sent four steers to the Point sale and got a very good price of £31-2-6 (Diary).

Another year, Frank McBride was the judge when I won. He was very impressed with my cattle, and would often bid on my cattle when they were being sold. The butchers would look and see Frank McBride bidding and think this must be a good deal, so they would start bidding, too. He could then pull out.

One year I bought a lot of cattle before a drought came. I sent some to grazing when it got too dry, but I thought I would put a few in the Temuka sale to see what I would get. Frank McBride bought them. After the sale, he came up to me and said "Don't put any more in the sale, till the drought breaks. I rescued you this time, but I won't be able to do it again". I was surprised that he had bidded, because I was just testing the market to see what I could get, but he saw himself as the protector of shorthorns, so he could not let them be sold cheap.

People looked on Hedley as a joke, but I did really well out of his cattle. He would send all his cattle down when he put the bulls out. Parira grew a lot of grass in the early summer, so the cattle improved my sheep and lambs. It was no use buying more ewes or lambs, as it would get dry in the later summer

Most people bought calves, but I preferred to buy yearlings. They often cost no more, but grew better, because they had been through their first winter.

Milking Cows

Mr Gainsford had milked three cows. He built a cowshed that had room to milk two cows. I was always amazed by his cows, as they were good milking cows with larger udders. Mr Saunders built the red cowshed. The dairy inspector was a friend and he helped him to build it. The old shed would not have passed the inspection necessary for selling cream.

I always kept a couple of cows and would milk them while Ellen prepared the breakfast. I enjoyed having some quiet time to think and plan the day.

The truck from the Waimate Dairy Coop would come around the district every Tuesday morning. It would pick up the full can of cream and leave an empty one. The cream cans had a number painted in red on them, so the factory knew where they came from. The driver would also leave the butter that Ellen had ordered. One of the older children would take the cream can out to the gate before school.

When we were supplying cream to the factory, the dairy inspector would come every few months and check the separator. He was really fussy about how it was washed. After running cold water through, I would break it down once a day and bring the stainless steel parts into the house. Ellen would wash then in cold water first and then in hot soapy water. Sometimes one of the children would take the parts out to the dairy and assemble it again.

In the early days, the separator had to be turned by hand. A little bell in the back would stop dinging, when it was spinning fast enough. Sometimes one of the older children would turn the handle. It would take ten minutes to separate the milk from two cows. The cream would be tipped into a cream can in the pantry. One of the children would take the buckets of skim milk and feed the calves. They often helped with bringing in the cows and washing down the yard when milking was complete at night.

I went to Levels Valley for a cow in December 1950 and paid £15 for her. One cow was called Aussie, because she had a map of Australia on her back. She died a few years later when she fell down behind the haybarn. Meg and Pansy were Friesian cows. Molly was a really good-natured Jersey cow.

Wild Cow

Darky was a really wild one. I bought her from a man near Fairview. Ronald and I went down with a horse float one evening to get her. When the man put her on a rope, she went berserk, but the man assured us she would calm down once she was in the float. We had a real struggle to get her on. As we were driving down the road, I looked out and saw her climbing out the back of the horse float. We stopped quickly and I grabbed a stake from the side of the road and hit her on the head to get her back in. She proved to be a terrible cow. She could jump over any fence, so we would never know where we would find her. The children hated milking her when I was sick. They were pleased when I got rid of her.

She went too far when she turned on me in 1962. We were going to the Fairlie show, so I went out early while it was still dark to milk the cows. I saw that Darky had calved, so decided to grab the calf while I could. I was carrying it into the cowshed, when the calf bellowed. Darky heard the noise, and charged and knocked me to the ground. I had a very narrow escape because she pushed me under the fence. I was able to crawl behind the big Macrocarpa tree, where she could not see me. Ellen heard the cow bellowing and came out to see what had happened. I told here to stay away. Eventually, the cow went back out into the paddock and I was able to come inside. I was very badly bruised and very sore, but it did not stop me from going to the show.

Seasons

1948 was quite a good season with a very mild winter and early spring. The summer had been very dry with seven inches less rain than in 1947.

1949 was another very good season. The early summer was dry, but the rain came in time to save us from a bad drought. According to the diary "we have many things to be thankful for".

45

In September 1950, I purchased a new suit and sports clothes. A few months later the wool was sold for a record price 8/6 a pound. The wool check was £2440.

> The year was a very prosperous one and we have many things to be thankful for. Prices for both meat and wool reached record heights and lambs were the heaviest we have ever sold (Diary)

The tallies for 1952 were as follows.

Paddock	Ewes	Lambs
Longridge	112	158
Cabbage Tree	114	181
Kowhai	104	140
Cliff	72	100
Pari	77	106
Ruapuna Flat	46	67
Middle Flat	80	110
Flat	86	112

280 sets of twins were tailed and over 1000 lambs in all. This was a big increase over the 446 in 1946. These were very good years to be farming.

1955 was a very good year, but it ended very dry. At the end of January 1956, 2 inches of rain came at night. The rain was very welcome, ending the driest year since 1931-32.

The weather for 1958 was very unusual. The first two months were wet and then it came dry and kept dry until the middle of November when 4 inches of rain fell over two weeks. The winter was frosty and the frosts kept right on through the spring and growth was very slow. The lambing was a record with 1800 lambs tailed.

> The past year (1958) has been one of ups and downs, but there are many bright spots and many things to be thankful for. I never thought it would be possible to go through the lambing with so little feed. Mother passed away peacefully on 15 Nov. While a gap is left in our lives, I am so thankful she had good health at the end (Diary).

1959 was a good one in many ways. The farm was very short of rain and very dry until the end of October, but after that there was a nice amount of rain. There was a terrible plague of porina and grass grub, which combined with the drought, left the paddocks in a very weak state. Feed was short in the spring and the lambs were not as good as they should have been. I sold the cull ewe lambs to Jim Risk at very low prices, but it was good to be rid of them as drought was getting severe. I had learned the wisdom of selling stock early, when Cannington started to get dry.

Grass grub and porina did enormous damage over the next few years and proved to be very difficult to control. Initially, DDT was very effective against them, but it was soon banned. The Silent Spring by Rachael Carson had an influence on thinking about DDT.

Storms and Floods

Life at Parira was often made trying by storms and floods. The Pareora River was just over the road from the house. A creek flowed round behind it and ran into the river about a hundred yards below the house. In March 1949, a strong gale blew at night. Next day Alister and I had to shift a tree that had fallen across the track and repair the roof of the cowshed and tie down an oat stack. A bad flood in April 1951 did a lot of damage to bridges.

After blowing a norwest gale all night, the weather turned to a cold southerly wind and rain on the morning of 24 September 1952. By 11 am, it was snowing and there were five inches of snow on the ground by 4 pm. The snow had cleared off the sunny facings by the next afternoon. There were very small losses in lambs in spite of the cold, but a lot of ewes went down with milk fever.

When I was growing up, the river had always been over on the other side of the riverbed. There was a big lagoon out in front of Parira, fed by a spring. It was about 3 feet deep and quite long. The spring water made it too cold to swim in, but we sometimes rowed a boat that Uncle Jack built.

A bad flood on 2 December 1952 went right through the lagoon and destroyed it. Most of the bridges on the Pareora River were damaged. The river washed into the road in front of our house. The council came in and built big stone groins to protect the road.

47

For the next twenty years, the river was on our side of the riverbed and caused many problems. When serious damage was done, the Catchment Board would come and plant willow trees. A pile driver powered by a traction engine drove railway irons into the ground first and they were connected together by wire ropes. A bulldozer would dig a trench to plant the willow trees. The willow trees were then tied to the wire rope, so they could not be washed away. This provided good protection, but it had to be extended whenever the river broke through in a new place.

In 1956, we had very heavy rain on the afternoon of the Sunday two days before Christmas. The creek rose in flood to a record height. I had cut hay in the Middle Flat. It seemed that the hay washed up against the fence and dammed up the creek. When the gates burst open, the creek came down in an enormous torrent. For a few moments the water lapped on the back doorstep of the house, but thankfully it did not come in through the door. However, it ran through the garden and orchard straight into the river, leaving a terrible mess of shingle, silt and hay all across Ellen's garden. The flood also broke down three fences and scoured the worked paddocks

On 15 September 1959, a strong norwest gale blew all night. It blew the roof off our implement shed, some in great big chunks. Some of the pieces of iron were away up on the Sunny Facing. That night the Nesscroft house burnt down. John Stevens had been burning stumps and the wind fanned the fire back to life while he was away. The fire brigade came from Pleasant Point, but by the time it got there, the house was almost gone. Mr Kenton put the roof back onto the implement shed in November, as it was covered by insurance.

Weeds and Insects

When I was young, barley grass was rare and caused few problems. As the soil became more fertile and grazing patterns changed, it became a serious weed. The seeds would damage the skins of our lambs, causing the pelts to be down-graded.

Nodding thistles also came quite late. They had been brought into NZ for sheepfeed. They were sown in the McKenzie country and spread across the country from there. We spent a lot of time and money spraying and grubbing Nodding Thistles. I got the blacksmith at Holmes Station to make a special adze with a narrow blade that could cut out a thistle without damaging the grass around it. The older children often helped with grubbing thistles, but it was a job they hated.

Rabbits became a bit of a problem on the riverbed. The Rabbit board dealt with this by dropping poisoned carrots from a plane. This was never very successful, but it kept them under control. On one occasion the Rabbit Board was burning gorse on the Riverbed up by Campbell's. They did not notice the power lines and melted them. Replacing the line proved to be quite expensive because the long span across the river used special wire. There was a dispute over who should pay, but in the end the Rabbit Board paid the cost.

Conferences and Field Days

I wanted to be a progressive farmer, so I was always keen to learn more about farming. I took every opportunity to attend field days and conferences, as they were a good opportunity to keep up with the latest ideas. According to the diary, these are some that I attended.

> Federated Farmers conference with Mr Rich - June 1948
>
> Lectures in Timaru with Eric Hall, Alister, and Keith Crawford - August 1948
>
> Levels with Alister and Norman - August 1948.
>
> Field day at Bakers and Darlings -1949
>
> Lincoln College with Campbells - 30/11/50
>
> YFC tractor safety course – June 1952
>
> Pasture conference and field day at Frank Clarke's (3 days) - November 1952
>
> Shearing demonstration by Godfrey Bowen - 1953
>
> Silorater demonstration - November 1954
>
> Field day at Norman Wrefords - November 1955
>
> Al and I went to Lincoln College with Alister - November 1957

Field days at Ashley Dene with Bill Wright - October 1959

Farm conference - June 1966

Field Day at Langley Downs with Ronald - June 1967

Horses

I used Mum's team at first, but added some horses to it. Alister and I shared the team, and in fine weather, we would make sure it was working every day, except when we were shearing or harvesting. This was a big help as I did not have to buy implements. It also gave me time for other things, whereas many teamsters spent their whole lives just driving their team. There was less sheep work in those days as there was no foot-rotting or drenching to do.

When I started farming, draught horses were very cheap, because people were changing to tractors. I bought a good horse at Hyland's clearing sale for £2. I bought another at a sale complete with a harness for £2. Jim Campbell did not like the way it held its head, but Mr Howell said it does not matter how a horse holds its head, if it costs just £2.

I really enjoyed working with horses and was good with them. Len Saunders often had trouble with his horses. They would jib and he would not be able to get them started. I would quietly climb up on the dray and speak to them firmly and they would start off again.

When tractors came in, men from the North Island came and bought all the horses. Dairy farmers wanted them for pulling joggers.

Joe

After the war, good hacks were very scarce, because the army had bought up all the spare horses. I wanted a new hack, so I phoned Jack Newbegin the agent at St Andrews and asked him to find me an unbroken horse. He could not find an unbroken one, but he said that he knew of one that had been broken, but had got out of hand. I could have it, if I could handle it. It was well bred, by Akron the New Zealand pacing champion out of a thoroughbred mare. The horse was at Joe Gibson's down on the Southburn road. The price was £10, so I decided to buy it. The agent promised that if I went down, Joe would have it ready for me.

I took my saddle and caught the bus to town, but got off at Gibson's place. Joe Gibson had been a friend of Dad's when he lived up at Mount Nimrod. He used to do all the docking of horses around the district, so I knew him slightly. Joe's son had something wrong with one leg and walked with a limp. Joe bought this fine-looking horse in and told the boy to "get on the pony and trot him around the paddock for a while and warm him up". I was a bit surprised because when the agent said he would be ready, I thought that he had meant that it would be ready for me to ride home.

Joe Gibson had the horse on the end of a length of clothesline. He asked me if I could ride and I said "Yes!" "Well", he said, "You get on". The moment that I got into the saddle, the horse started to buck. He bucked and bucked. Fortunately, he did not move, but just bucked on one spot. Somehow, I stuck to the saddle until he calmed down. I did not get off again, because I thought that if I got off, I might not get on again.

I decided to head for home. Going past Evan's farm, I saw a cast sheep in the paddock. That was the only time in my life that I went past a cast sheep without stopping and picking it up, but I dared not get off. I eventually arrived home safely. The next day I took

51

Joe out onto the riverbed among the big boulders to get on. I knew he wouldn't buck there, because it would be too hard on his feet. He only ever bucked once again. I was on the road talking to Norman Crawford, when the dogs started fighting and he got a fright. He stood on the spot and bucked, so I managed to stick on him.

Joe turned out to be a marvellous horse with a great amble. Ambling was a type of pacing that allowed you to sit without posting off the saddle. I tested him out once against a tractor, and he could amble at about 7 mph. An average horse would walk about four miles in an hour, so his amble was a great advantage. Joe was very comfortable to ride. I used to love riding him with other people, because I could always out-distance them when walking. They would slowly drift back and would have to break into a jog to keep up with my walk. This used to annoy Jim Campbell, because he bought a flash horse about the same time, but it was not a good walker, and I could walk away from him.

When I was shearing and Uncle Jack was staying with Mum, he used to ride Joe around the sheep. I never told him how Joe bucked and he used to call him a "real gentleman". I kept Joe until he was done.

One day I tied Joe to a gate in the Top Flat. While I was doing something, he pulled on the reins and lifted the gate off its hinges. The gate gave him a fright, so he bolted. Eventually, the reins parted from the gate and he calmed down. The gate was smashed and Joe's leg was hurt, but he healed up quickly.

Later I bought Neil Macaulay from Roy Glidden. He was a great horse for working cattle. He could cut one out and it would not be able to beat him.

Rod

When I retired to Barnes Street, Alison Baker got me involved with Riding for the Disabled. I really enjoyed working with horses again. It was great seeing the children develop their riding skills.

The Jogger

Most Canterbury farmers used a sledge for doing small jobs. I saw a picture in the paper of a jogger being used on a dairy farm and thought it was a good idea. I went to town and found an old car with a truck deck that was for sale for £5.00. I offered the man £4.00, if he would tow me out to Saltwater Creek, as it was not registered. He agreed, so I drove it home and made it into a jogger. The jogger was great because it could be pulled by one horse, whereas a sledge needed two horses. I was the only person in the district to use a jogger. It was great for feeding out hay in the winter when the paddocks were wet, and the tractor would make a mess. Alan Smith bought the engine from the truck to drive his shearing plant.

Bell was the first horse to pull the jogger. Later Bloss took over this task.

In 1948 Alister and I built a hay cart. The idea was to have something lower than a dray or a wagon on which to carry hay, as they were very high to load. The hay cart had wheels on the back and skids on the front. It did not work very well, because it was difficult to turn. It sat out in front of the old haybarn for many years. Later I used it while pouring molasses onto poor quality hay.

Better Equipment

Tractors

Eventually, I had to change from horses to tractors. Alister and I bought a second hand McCormick T20 from Mr Powell at Waihaorunga for £500 in March 1951. It was very slow and could pull no faster than the team of horses, but it could turn quicker. T20s were very common around Cannington. They had steering clutches and a kerosene motor. They had to be cranked, but they would always start.

I bought a new petrol Nuffield wheel tractor in partnership with Alister for £766 in July 1951. During the next few months, drawbars were put onto all the farm implements, so they could be pulled by the tractor. I bought a big drill to go on the workshop wall and a set of stocks and dies to assist with this work. The dray was done first, and then the seed drill and the roller.

The tractor did not pull very well at first, because it did not have enough traction. Mr King brought out some steel grips and they helped, but they were awkward because they had to be unbolted and rotated out to be effective. A tyre once blew out on the Nuffield while I was working on the Top Flat. The tyres were full of water for weight, so I got a bit of a shower and arrived home very wet.

By 1954, the Nuffield needed a valve grind. This was a regular requirement for motors in those days. The following year Trevor Stewart fitted it with new rings.

A new David Brown crawler tractor and set of offset discs were purchased in November 1953. The David Brown proved to be a high maintenance tractor. It ran on petrol and was very fuel hungry, going through two gallons an hour. Two years after we bought it, Trevor had to fit new rings. The following year the tracks needed new bushes. In 1959, we sent the David Brown into town to be repaired. A few months later, we had a mechanic out to repair it again. When Tractor Services put in a second-hand diesel engine, it went much better. It was overhauled again in 1973.

I bought a TEA Fergusson tractor for £60 in 1958. It had a tray on the back that was good for carting hay and sheep. This replaced the jogger and sledge.

Farm Machinery

When I started farming at Parira, we mostly used Mum' machinery, but over the years I slowly bought my own equipment. The first purchase was a horse-drawn mower at Amyes clearing sale. I spent the next two days repairing it. The power to drive the mower came from the steel wheels, so if it got jammed, it was hard to get going again. I bought a topdresser for £30 in 1952. This was horse-drawn, but later I fitted a drawbar, so it could be pulled with a tractor.

Alister and I brought a mower to go on the Nuffield. It broke down the second time we used it. It was bolted underneath the tractor, and this made it too rigid, so if it hit something, the mower would break. The pitman also seemed to break frequently.

Once we owned a wheel tractor, I needed a trailer. I went to a sale at Cricklewood and bought a trailer for £46. It had been made from a truck deck by Mr Barr. This trailer was used on Parira for many years. The front was very heavy, so it took two people to lift it on to the tractor drawbar. Alan eventually developed a method of lifting it with the hydraulic arms on the tractor.

In 1962, I bought a Cambridge roller from Mick Sugrue for £100. It had a seedbox on the back that could be used for broadcasting seed. Previously, we had borrowed Baker's roller when sewing grass seed.

Better Tractors

When it was time to replace the Nuffield, Alister and I disagreed. Alister wanted another Nuffield, but I thought they were too light and narrow to pull well. We did buy a new Nuffield, but it was no better, so the following year, I bought a new Massey Ferguson 65 tractor and traded in the TEA Ferguson. The new tractor had differential lock, dual rear wheels and good hydraulics. I also bought a new three-furrow Clough plough and a grubber to use with it. These implements did not have a land wheel, so the tractor hydraulics transferred the weight of the implement onto the back wheels of the tractor.

This new tractor could pull very well. Alan and Ronald became very skilled at driving it and were able to cultivate most of the hilly paddocks on the farm. They could handle ground that most people in the district would have worked with a crawler tractor. Doing this work with a wheel tractor was a big saving. With the diff lock on, that tractor would almost go anywhere.

Our method of cultivation was to grub the paddock three or four times, working at a different angle each time. If the ground still needed further breaking down, we would run the discs over it. Then it would be harrowed a couple of times with the grub harrows and then a couple with the tine harrows to get a good seed bed. In 1964, I went to Mr Ward's sale and bought a set of grub harrows for £42. We used these extensively when cultivating the paddocks.

Farm Workers

The first man I employed at Parira was Paul Oudemans. He was Dutch, but had immigrated from Indonesia. He started in 1953 and was paid £33-3-0 per month on the last Thursday of the month. Tax of £2-17-0 was deducted from his wages. Paul stayed for two years, but he was not really suited to farm work.

Jack Arnst came in 1955, but it did not work really well and he only stayed for a year. I only took him on to please Don Neale, and it was not a good move. He had been the tractor driver at Craigmore, and there were always plenty of men there. He tended to watch what others were doing, rather than see what needed to be done and get stuck in. He was only really happy when driving the tractor. He left when he bought some land down near Pleasant Point. The Arnsts had two boys and two girls about the same age as our family. Margaret and Barbara were later drowned on Lake Tekapo in a terrible boating accident.

Trevor Stewart started working for me in 1956. His mother was a widow, and he had been working on farms since he was a boy. He was the best man I had, as he could turn his hand to anything. He had worked a bit as a mechanic and was very good with motors. He did up an old motorbike and rode to work on it. I did not expect him to do any sheep work, because I liked doing that myself. I just wanted him to do the tractor work. He stayed for nearly three years.

The next person was John Davies, who came at the end of 1958 and stayed for two years. He was a bit of a disappointment. I had always made a stipulation with men that they start at 7.30 am. I did this so they would be at work by 8 am. With John, because he was Christian, I said to start at 8 am, thinking that he would have the tractor out and in the paddock by then, but John would be driving in the gate right on 8 am. The Davies left in August 1960. I then managed on my own until Alan left school at the end of 1961.

Crops

In the first few years, I grew quite a few different crops. Cropping was a good way for a farmer to earn some extra cash. The first crop was ryegrass on the Top Flat. Jim Calder harvested it with his header, but it was a poor crop, producing only 16 bags of grass seed.

In 1947 we had oats on the top of the Windmill Paddock and the Flat. They were tall and tangled and very hard to reap, but the crops were good and we built six stacks. The mill came in April and harvested them. I think this was the last time a threshing mill came to Parira. By then it was getting very difficult to get a mill and if you were able to get one, it did not have good men working on it, because most of the experienced men had gone off to the war and had not returned.

I grew oats in the Middle Ridge and the Top Flat in the summer of 1948. They were used for chaff.

In January 1949, I reaped and stacked a crop of H1 ryegrass on the Longridge. It was threshed a few days later by forking the sheaves directly into a header. Jock Blackmore would drive the header along the rows of stooks. We would cut the string off the sheaves, as we fed them onto the platform of the header. This was the best crop that I ever had and earned my biggest cheque. We used some of the proceeds to buy the truck. The straw was stacked for hay. Les Gray brought around a hay sweep and Pat and Frank Casey provided assistance.

No crop was grown in 1950, but the next year, we harvested H1 grass seed on the Top Flat. Norman came and helped with the stooking. We also direct headed a small area for grass seed. I was still growing oats for chaff, but this was probably the last year that chaff was needed.

In 1952, a crop of white clover was harvested. Clover had to be harvested directly. McCormack clover shellers could also be used to harvest clover. A chains stripper would sometimes go up the road to Whiterock about that time. This would collect browntop seed to be used for sowing lawns.

In 1954, my grass seed yielded 225 bags. In 1956, Andy Scott headed our oats. It was a good crop. At the end of that year, Alister and I bought an Allis Chalmers header in partnership with Bill Wright. One tractor was not enough during the harvest time, so I hired a tractor and Jack Kleim drove it out from Timaru.

The harvest in 1961 was terrible. I had shut the Phalaris Paddock up for a crop of ryegrass. In the middle of January, Jock Blackmore cut it with his binder. I preferred the binder to a mower as the grass fell the other way, leaving the seed head protected. It also fed into the header better. That night it started to rain and it continued for four days. A week after the rain stopped, we tried to start heading in the afternoon, but it was too dull to make much progress.

The Allis Chalmers would block up if the crop was damp. It only had a 6-foot wide platform, so it was very slow. One man stood on the back and sowed the bags by hand when they were full. Andy Scott came the next afternoon with his 12-foot self-propelled header to help. He worked on the other half of the paddock. The next day a strong norwester blew. Andy was heading in the morning. Al and I started in the afternoon and made good progress until the header broke down. The next afternoon it rained again, and the rest of the crop was ruined by the weather. We only managed to harvest 100 bags of ryegrass in total.

We had a great deal of difficulty getting rid of the straw. We managed to bale some, but the rest was so soggy that we could not bale or burn it. In the end, I had to push it over the back facing with a hay sweep. A month later when we were harvesting wheat, the header broke down on the second afternoon.

Chaffcutter

In 1948, we had run out of chaff before the chaff cutter arrived in June, so I borrowed chaff from Norman. When the chaff cutter came, we got 330 bags. I sold 30 bags to Alex McPherson and returned the chaff I had borrowed to Norman.

In 1950, I worked on the chaff cutter while it was at Casey's in the afternoon. When it came to Greenridge the next day, I helped again. We had to sledge the chaff up the cutting, because it was too wet for the trucks to come down. Mr Hawthorrne carted the chaff from the top of the hill. The same problem occurred in 1951, but we pulled the trucks out with the tractor.

Hay

In 1951, I went to town and then to Seadown to find Jack Kleim. He came with a sweep and elevator and helped with the hay-making. Jim Campbell was helping as well. We built the stack in the traditional way.

The next year, I borrowed a hay sweep from Riddles to help Campbell's stack their hay. I got a bit of a fright, as the tractor slipped over a bank. I jumped off, as I expected it to tip over, but it idled slowly down the hill, so I was able to climb on the back and stop it. However, the hay sweep was damaged. We repaired the sweep and finished Campbell's hay the next day.

Hedley Squire had the first baler in the district. It was a Case and used wire to bind the bales. The wire was a nuisance, as no matter how careful you were, some ended up on the paddocks. Also, if the hay heated, the wire would corrode and break.

Hedley converted the baler to use twine. Two men sat on the back. One would push the divider through between the bales. The person on the other side would grab the twine cut it and tie the bale. Timing was important. If the divider was pulled back too soon, the twine would twist, and the other person could tie the strings wrong and two bales would be joined together. This was hot, dusty work.

Hedley soon tired of baling, but he would lend me the baler. Later he sold it to me. Alister and I bought a new Case baler with mechanical knotters that tied the twine automatically in 1956. This was a great step forward, as the baling could be done by one man.

The Case baler had two problems. The needles went from side to side rather than from top to bottom as on other balers. This caused the baler to produce banana shaped bales, if the hay was unfit. The baler was powered with an air-cooled V4 Wisconsin engine. They were great motors, when they were going, but could be temperamental to start, especially when hot. Many times, I wore my knuckles thin, cranking it on a hot day. We generally found it best to just leave the motor running, once it was going. We sometimes took the belt off the big flywheel and put it onto the pulley on the Farmall tractor and turned the engine, until it started.

We bought an International baler from Donald Simpson in 1972. This ran off the tractor power take-off, so we did not have to worry about starting a motor.

Hay Barn

I was one of the first farmers in the district to build a hay barn. Due to war restrictions, it was almost impossible to get materials. The larch poles were advertised in the paper. They were not ideal, because they were not treated, but there was nothing better available. I tendered for a blue gum tree on the side of the road near Cave. My tender was successful, so Jim Calder helped split the tree up into planks to be used for rafters. I had seen tar drums used for roofing on a shed down near Fairview. I was able to get some drums from the city council. I paid the council 2/- per drum to cut the ends out. They had to be flattened out, so I borrowed Evan Riddle's big roller to get them really flat. We turned the long edges up, and alternated them when nailing them to the rafters, so they would be waterproof.

In May 1947, a bulldozer came to level the ground where it would be built. Uncle Jack did a lot of the building work. He put up the first of the larch poles in July. By November, we were standing on the stacked hay to put on the roof. The hay barn was exposed to the south, so Uncle Jack put a timber wall on the southern side in 1953, leaving trapdoors for the hay slide.

The hay slide was a revolutionary idea. I built the slide out of the long wooden poles that Mr Gainsford had used for his radio aerial. A truck of hay could be driven up the hill behind the hay barn to the top of the slide. The hay bales would then slide down into the hay barn.

The transport workers loved the slide, because the hay barn was quite high, so it would have been really hard work if the bales had to be lifted up into the top of the barn. However, there was a catch.

The hill up to the top of the hayslide got quite steep, so an inexperienced truck driver could jerk his truck, causing half of the load to full off the back onto the ground. The bales would then have to be carried by hand up to the top of the slide. A driver seldom made this mistake twice.

If the hay was not very fit, the bales would not slide well. When this happened, one of the children would be called in to help. They would stand by the slide and give the bales a push to send them on their way down into the barn. This was fun for a while, but it soon got monotonous.

Later, we built a Cyclone hay barn out on the flat in front of the Hillview cottage. Lester Hill, Frank Casey and Alan all worked on it. John Ramage and Lester started putting the roof on hay barn and Ronald and Alan finished it.

Good Lucerne Hay

Mr Gainsford was the first person in the district to grow Lucerne. It did really well on the river flats, but making good hay was a real problem. Most people just let hay make itself, but I wanted to do something to improve the process. I read in an English magazine about a farmer who made his hay in one day. He would cut and crush it early in the morning, turn it frequently and bale it that night. Turning allowed the air to get through, which dried it quicker.

I could not buy a crusher, so I bought an old farmerator (forage harvester) for haymaking in 1962. I had seen one demonstrated for making silage back in 1955. The one he bought had rubber paddles with blades on the end. Once it was blunted by the stones, it bruised the Lucerne well. I found I could make Lucerne hay in two days. I would mow it early in the morning and followed with the forage harvester. I would then turn it frequently to allow the air to flow through it. I would be able to bale it the next evening. This allowed us to make really good hay.

Crimpers were available, but they damaged the Lucerne too much and the leaf would fall off as it dried. One day I saw a roller hay crusher advertised in the paper. It had been used as a demonstrator, but was nearly new. It was 7 ft, which was a little too wide, but otherwise perfect. I bought an old Fordson tractor and put a belly mower on it, so I could pull the crusher behind it. This made a very efficient system. The crusher had a hard rubber roller on top and a steel roller with ¾ inch square grooves on the bottom. It bruised the stalks enough to make them dry quickly, but left lots of leaf on the Lucerne hay.

I needed an efficient way to turn the hay frequently, so I bought an old Farmall A tractor to pull the hay rake. It was funny to look at because the motor was set to one side, but it could turn very sharply. The Bamford finger wheel rake was gentle on the Lucerne.

Carting Hay

In the early days, Alister and I carted most of the hay using two drays. We would each load our own dray, which was hard as they were high off the ground. Although Alister was shorter than me, he was very strong.

Later we used the Cave Transport to cart the hay as they would cart it in the evening that it was baled. I had a principle that I would never bale hay if I could not cart it in that night. If hay got wet in the row, you could dry it, but once in the bale, drying wet hay was hopeless. I would never bale more hay than we could cart in that day.

The Cave Transport was quite expensive and I could not always get them when I wanted them, so in 1961 I also bought a SAM hay loader from Brown Wood Motors that went on the side of the truck. It detached from the truck and with the "nose" removed, could be used as an elevator at the shed.

We took a while to learn how to use the SAM. The boys would often help to drive the truck, while one of the men stacked the hay. At first, a lot of bales were chopped in half, but the boys soon became very good operators and could pick up a bale even it was at right angles or tipped on its side. One man and a boy could load a truck quite quickly on their own.

We then put the SAM onto the old Bedford Truck, so we were not dependent on the Cave Transport. In 1962, we bought a second Bedford truck with a slightly longer deck at the Farmers Garage for £150. This gave two trucks for carting hay. We would carry in a hundred bales on each truck. We would stack in four loads in the hay barn. We would leave the last two loads in the trucks and put them in the hay barn in the morning. In this way, we could get 600 bales done each day. After unloading the hay, we would cut some more for the next day.

In 1970, I bought an Austin truck from Farmers Garage for $400. It was painted yellow and brown, because it had been used as a coal delivery truck. This enabled us to put the oldest Bedford to rest.

Sometimes when we were making hay, a norwester would come up. If we raked the hay up into big rows for the baler, it would blow away. We would try to rake the hay just in front of the baler, so it could pick it up before the wind caught it. The driver of the tractor pulling the rake had to be alert to avoid being hit by the baler.

If the wind was really strong, or the hay was too dry, we would wait till it went down at night. In 1961, I started baling Alister's hay at 9.30 pm and did not get finished until midnight.

Silage

Parira always produced an enormous amount of grass in the early summer, when the weather was too unsettled for making hay. I wanted to find a way to make better use of it, so I experimented with making silage. The first attempt to make silage was in 1952. I went to town and bought a buck rake, which I used to build a small pit of Lucerne silage in the creek opposite Riverbank. I was held up with a puncture in the tractor tyre while working on the silage pit. This experiment was not a success. The Lucerne silage was unpalatable for the sheep and most of it rotted.

In 1956, I tried another method on the Middle Flat. Our new Case baler would bale short bales of unfit hay. Bill Wright pulled the baler with his Landrover, and we carted the bales into a silage heap by a bank. This process did not work either.

I tried vacuum pack silage for the first time in 1970. A plastic sheet went underneath and another on the top. The two sheets were then sealed by pressing a tube into an open plastic pipe. The first heaps were on the Middle Ridge and Coopers Flat. Gary Stocker helped make this with his forage harvester. This method made good silage,

65

but it was hard to keep the packs sealed. The wind would tear the sheet or grass would prick it, and air would get in, causing the silage to rot. We found that crushing the Lucerne made silage more palatable for sheep.

Alan and Ronald would go and load the truck up with silage each evening and we would feed it out in the morning. This was the first time we made silage that the sheep would eat.

Gary Stocker was the first to buy a chopper to make haylage. We bought a JF chopper for haylage in shares with Alan and Graham Kirk in 1977. It chopped the green material up, making it easy to feed out. We would wilt it for a day, to get most of the moisture out. We then put the haylage in a pit with concrete sides and roll it really hard with a big tractor to get all the air out. If it was rolled hard, there would be no waste. We would cover it with a plastic sheet to keep out the rain. The heaps were covered with hundreds of old tyres to keep the sheet from blowing off. Haylage was a really effective method of storing grass for winter feed.

I bought a trailer that fed the haylage out automatically. We could use the same trailer when harvesting haylage. The tractors had automatic drawbars, so we could change trailers automatically, without getting off the tractor. If the weather was fine, we would make haylage all night, as it did not have to be dry. A Kirk-Rowley-McKenzie partnership bought a big Krone wind-rower in 1978, as a standard mower could not cut the grass fast enough to keep ahead of the chopper. It also eliminated the need to rake the hay up into big rows.

Fencing

Many fences had to be renewed with concrete posts replacing the old native wooden posts that had rotted away. In 1953, I bought a new post hole digger that fitted on the back of the tractor. This made the task easier, but the auger had to be lifted out by winding a hand winch. Later when the tractors had hydraulics, we modified the digger to be lifted by the tractor.

When digging posts on the flats, we would often strike a big boulder that had to be dug out by hand. Once the post holes were dug, we would ram the soil tight around the concrete post by hand. Many of the fences were made with high tensile cyclone netting.

In the 1970s, we started driving in tanalised wooden posts with a tractor-driven post driver. This made fencing an easier task, and the post hole digger was a thing of the past. In 1977, I bought post hole borer in partnership with Alister Rowley. This allowed a lighter post to be driven in by hand.

Water

Cannington could get very dry and droughts were a problem because there was not much water on the farm. When the Timaru pipeline was put in, the City Council had a fairly casual engineer. He gave everyone on the Cliffs Rd the right to take unlimited water from the pipeline. I don't think the Council would have allowed it, if they had known what would happen. Later on, I could see the possibility of putting in troughs for my stock, so I wrote to the Council asking for permission to extend the pipe. They did not look into it, but approved my request. I piped water onto the flats and up into each of the gullies. I used a sight along a spirit level to decide how high I could go. I later did the same on Calder's place. Now, most paddocks had good water for the stock. This was a tremendous benefit, as we had been dependent on dams, which dried up during the summer.

The first pipes were put in during 1953, using a mole plough borrowed from McKerchars. Uncle Jack helped me. We pulled the plough with the crawler tractor. We first dug a ditch the length of a piece of galvanised pipe. When one piece of pipe had been pulled into the hole, we would stop and join another length of pipe on. The plough had a very sharp blade. On one occasion, I dropped the blade and jammed my finger. I had to go to the doctor and could not work for a couple of days. Once the pipes were in the ground, the troughs had to be connected.

The house always depended on the Timaru Water supply. Our tank was only forty gallons on the roof of the house, so we quickly ran out of water if the intake at the dam up in the gorge got blocked by a flood. When the Timaru City got a new reservoir, they tended to turn the water off for longer, so in 1963, we installed a big concrete tank on the hill above the house. This provided a more certain supply of water for our home.

During the winter, if care was not taken, the pipes would freeze. In the evening, I would look outside, and if the night looked frosty, I would go and turn the water off by the road and turn on a tap in the trough in the yard. This would drain the pipes, so they would not freeze. In the morning, when the sun had come up, someone would go out and turn the water on again. With this method, we almost never had frozen pipes.

In 1976, the Canningon-Motukaika water scheme put water to all farms in the area. This freed us from dependence on the Timaru water supply.

Aerial Topdressing

During the 1950s, aerial topdressing became a big thing in New Zealand. We often topdressed the back facings of the Kowhai, Pari and Cliff Paddocks from the air. The first plane to come was a Tiger Moth. It landed on Gerry's ridge. The pilot forgot to take some rope out of the hopper, and when he took off with the first load, he could not get the hopper to open. He landed with a full load, breaking the tail skid. They had to take the skid to Timaru for repairs, before they could finish their work.

Subsequent planes were Austers. They flew off the Longridge, because it was higher up. Often the man who drove the loader would arrive at the airstrip in the fertiliser hopper. Eric Gawler was a popular pilot. Like many of the pilots he had been in the air force during the war, so was quite daring. When topdressing on Cooper's Flat, he flew under the power lines, rather than going up over them.

By the end of the 1960s, aerial topdressing was getting too expensive and was replaced by four-wheel drive trucks that could spread fertiliser on steep paddocks. They had big blowers that could push fertiliser down over the back facings.

Sheds

Mr Gainsford built the woolshed when he first arrived. It was very small and only held about 100 sheep, so keeping sheep dry for shearing was always a struggle. There was a room at the back for the oil engine that drove the shearing machines. The fumes from the oil engine made working in the woolshed quite unpleasant. The grinder for sharpening cutters and combs was kept in the engine room.

On the side of the woolshed was a room that we called the oil shed. This was where Mr Gainsford kept the batteries for his first lighting system. He must have had a wind-powered generator for charging the batteries, but I do not remember how it worked. Later he used this room as a toolshed and store for oil and grease.

The next shed round was an implement shed. Next to it was a small room, called the whare, where a man used to sleep. Later this became the feedhouse where Ellen kept the wheat and mash for the hens. The next room round was the dray shed. The whare was at the back of the dray shed. The dray shed later became the coal shed. The slightly bigger one next to it was the wagon shed. We later used this as a car shed. The chaff shed was next to the stable. It was transformed into an area for storing wool bales.

The stable was a lean-to on the road side of the woolshed. Once the horses were gone, I put down grating and built pens to expand the number of sheep that could be kept under cover in the woolshed to 200. I would put another 100 sheep under the big Macrocarpa tree, as it would keep them dry through a light shower of rain. Three hundred dry sheep would keep the shearers busy for most of a day.

Our woolshed was very hot, because the surrounding trees were quite close. We would open up all the doors and windows to try and get a breeze moving. If you climbed up on top of the stacked wool bales near the roof, it was really scorching.

Mr Gainsford had a large pigsty at the back of the orchard. The Saunders extended it into a large fowl house, as they had a lot of fowls. They also used the implement shed for hens and made the whare into a feed house. The old hut was brought in to replace the whare. I used the old pigsty as a workshop.

The sheep yards were also built by Mr Gainsford. I rebuilt them with timber planks, because they were mostly just netting and stakes and not good for working sheep. I worked on the sheep yards for nearly a month in 1951. The following year Uncle Jack built a footrot trough. I was very pleased with the trough when we used it for the first time.

Keith Crawford welded railway irons for a new implement shed in 1957 and Trevor Stewart built the shed during the winter.

Shearers

Alister and I did our own shearing for the first few years. The first independent shearers were Dave Chisholm and Peter Quigley who did the crutching in 1953. The following year, Peter Quigley and Ian Patterson did the shearing. One day when Peter was away, I shore with Ian in his place.

Ian was very strong, but he was a very greedy shearer to work with. I remember once working with him at Mr Crawford's. I always thought that even though you were a shearer, you should be a gentleman, but Ian was quite ruthless. He was strong and could push right into the back of the pen to get an easy shearing sheep. His mates would always end up with the tough ones.

Ian Paterson was still doing the shearing ten years later. Some of his mates were Claude Allan, Roger Maxwell, Quentin Ryan Peter Erwood and John McHaffie. By 1970, Bruce Stowell was assisting John McHaffie.

Shearing was hard work. The men would start at 7.30 am and work for two hours. They would break for thirty minutes and then work for another two hours. They would work the same pattern in the afternoon, finishing at 5.30 pm.

Fat Lamb Drafters

Archie Hutton, who had been very good to Mum, was eventually replaced by Bill Borrie, but he was not good for us. Bill was the old-type drafter, used to drafting big fat lambs. He never learned to draft lighter lambs. It was not until George Davidson came along that we saw how it should be done. At the same time, over-fats became a problem, because the freezing works would reject them, making them worthless. Sometimes we would go down to the freezing works and collect the rejected carcasses so that we could eat them ourselves. Picking out over-fat lambs was a skill that the drafters had to learn.

Bill Borrie was also very slow, but he was a friend of Ellen's family, so I stuck with him. He started drinking and making a mess of things. Alister got rid of him first, because all afternoon he was running around behind the poplar trees to have a leak. Alister was suspicious when he did not get as many lambs away as he expected, so he got another drafter to go through the mob again. They took a whole lot more lambs, so Alister never had Bill back again. I had to keep Bill on, because he looked upon himself as a family friend. I was glad when he retired.

When George Davidson started, the number of lambs that we got away went up dramatically. This was really important, as getting space at the works became more difficult as the summer went on and we needed to get our lambs away early before it got dry.

The drafter would always arrive at 6 am and I would have everything ready for him. I would have been up at daylight to get the sheep in. Working sheep was much easier early in the day, before the weather got too hot. After the drafter had been, we would have to dag them and later still they would have to be loaded on to the truck to go to the freezing works at Pareora. Drafting was a long tiring day, for men and dogs. The children would come out and help push the sheep up into the drafting race. Alister would pull a leafy branch off the poplar trees for them to whack the sheep on the backs. The rustling noise would keep the sheep moving.

71

When the Cave Transport came to pick up the lambs, the children would come out again to help load the truck. The lambs did not like walking up the temporary ramp, so many hands helped. The base of the ramp went under the truck. The sides hung on the side of the truck. They were taken down and clamped onto the base, so loading could start. The driver would put a specific number of lambs in each pen on the truck.

Dogs

I loved working with dogs, so I enjoyed dog trials. In 1946, I went to the Mt Nessing trials with Phil Green. In 1948, I got second in the handy with Boy and fourth in long pull with Mist at the YFC dog trials. Alister won the huntaway with Tip. The YFC held a dance at night. Later in the year, I sold Mist to Mr Darling for £8.

In 1954, Ring got second in the long pull at the Mt Nessing dog trials. I sold Val for £35 that year, too. Ring descended from old Boy. He was a marvellous dog, and he was still going well in 1960, when I got 1st in the handy and 2nd in the huntaway and long pull events and won Braeval cup (most points) at the YFC dog trials with him. Laddie was another descendant from Boy. He looked like a yellow Alsatian, but was a great dog. I later lent him to Donald Burnett at Mount Cook Station.

Later in 1960, I went to the Dog sale at Tinwald with Hamish McPherson and sold a handy dog Tip for £30-10. Selling dogs continued to be a good source of cash over many years, as many farmers did not know how to train a dog. As long as farmers drove in trucks or motorbikes, I knew there would be a demand for good working dogs. In 1969, I spoke to the Young Farmers Club about training a dog.

In 1966, I took Fly and Lassie to the vet because they were both very sick. He found they both had hepatitis. Fly was a huntaway that I had bought from Bill Mack. She was an ugly dog, but a tireless worker with a yelp of a bark. She loved to lie in the water trough and get totally wet. I fed both dogs a mixture of milk and eggs every day to try and build up their strength.

After a couple of weeks, Fly started eating a little meat. She gradually recovered and was the mother of Ruff, whom Ron trained. Unfortunately, when Lassie went back to the vet, she had to be destroyed as she was very weak. What a great little dog she was. She was also the mother of Boy, Alan's first dog, another very intelligent dog. I was sad to lose Lassie, as she was the best link to Boy and Ring.

Mr Williamson came out and vaccinated all our dogs against hepatitis and distemper. Cloud did not want to be vaccinated, so we had to stretch him out between two ropes so the vet could get near him. He did not understand that it was for his own good.

Don was a big black and tan, North Island huntaway. He was extremely hard to control, but he could work all day in the heat without faltering.

Alister

Alister and I always worked together, and we were great mates. We talked about everything and rarely disagreed. Shirley said that Alister only started talking to her about farming when they moved to Rosewill. Before that, he just talked every decision through with me. Alister would come down to Parira on many mornings. Ellen would call from the kitchen, "Al's here", and I would head out to work with him.

In 1963, Alister moved to Rosewill, marking the end of an era. I bought Riverbank from him for Alan for £3500. Norman Crawford brought Greenridge. This together with what he had bought from Pat Casey put the Priest's farm back together. I helped Alister to drive his sheep down to Rosewill. We had to drive down Mountain View road, which was getting quite built up. We had a great deal of fun keeping the sheep out of people's gardens. Alister and I also took their furniture and hen house down on the truck.

Alister left because, he was fed up with the river flooding, but after he left, the river moved back to the other side and ceased to be a problem. His new farm proved to be very dry, but he enjoyed having a farm that was not split into two blocks.

Life on Parira

Country Life (Ellen)

During the first few years at Parira, I had to take the bus when going to town. Aunt Helen was still living with Gran at Riverbank, so I would take Alan and Ronald up to Helen, and she would look after them while I was in town.

The NZR bus station was in Heaton Street. It was always a hard walk up the hill carrying the load of parcels that had been bought during the day. The day before Gran died, she had been to town. It was a very hot day, and she would have walked up that same hill.

The Cave Store delivered groceries twice a week. They would phone me on the previous day and take my order. They would also bring the mail and paper. On the days that groceries did not get delivered, the paper would come to the school, and be delivered by the school children going home from school.

The washhouse at Parira had only cold water. Each Monday I would boil up the copper to do the main washing. The washing had to be scrubbed on a washing board. Rod did not think a wringer was necessary, because his mother and Helen managed without one. They would wring the clothes out by hand. Helen was very strong, so it was easier for her. Rod must have relented, because he gave me a wringer as a birthday present in 1946.

On Monday while I had plenty of hot water, I would empty the bucket from the outdoor toilet. I would dig a hole somewhere in the garden and bury the waste. It had Jay's fluid in it, but this was still not a very pleasant task. I would use plenty of hot water to wash out the bucket before returning it to the toilet.

On Tuesdays, I would go over to the riverbed and gather gorse sticks for the copper fire. I would fill a sack and carry it back under my arm.

The kitchen had a wet back in the open fire and a small water cylinder with a tap on the side. If I had washing on other days of the week, I would carry a bucket of hot water from the kitchen out to the wash house. When I had babies, I would wash nappies every day by carrying water out there. The nappies would be boiled once a week in the copper.

I did most of the vegetable garden, because if I waited for the men, nothing got planted. In the early days, Uncle Jack gave me a lot of help in the garden.

The House (Rod)

The kitchen had an electric range when we moved into the house. The kitchen was on the cold side of the house, with only one window that got no sun. The open fireplace was poorly designed, and all the heat went up the chimney. There were four doors out of the room, so it was always cold. I remember Ellen wearing gloves to keep warm while sweeping the kitchen floor.

Several improvements were made to the house in 1946. A new electric stove was bought from the Power Board for £37-14. We also bought a new wireless. This was made of white plastic and was used in the woolshed when the family had grown up. Ellen bought a Singer sewing machine. Uncle Jack built a new meat-safe and helped move the fruit trees into the orchard. The bathroom was painted.

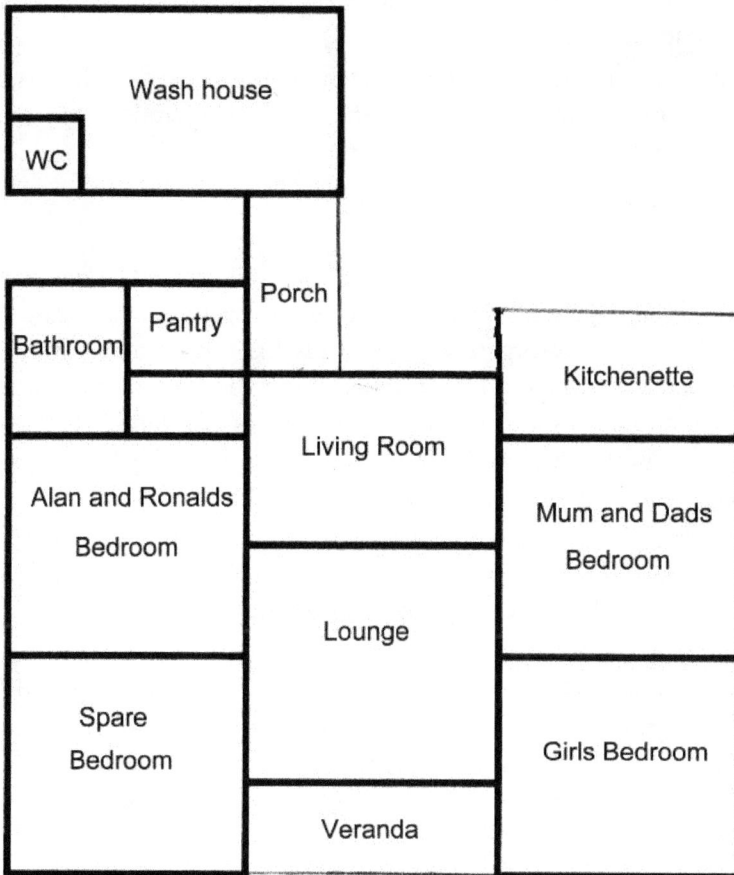

Mr Kenton came and refurbished the kitchen in June 1954, the year

Jean was born. He put in a kitchenette and turned the kitchen into a living room. Fortunately, it was not a cold winter, as the first thing that Mr Kenton did was to take out the kitchen window. The following week we took out the fireplace and carted the bricks away. The entire project took him a month and he left the Esse heater till last. The linoleum was not laid on the floor until the end of July. This was a great improvement, but the living room was still draughty and cold, because it had four doors and got no sun.

We had the outside toilet in the jungle until 1956. Mr Lawson came to mark out the drain for the septic tanks and Alister and I dug them out. Once the tank and the sump had been built, Mr Lawson came back and installed the toilet.

Ellen painted and wall-papered each of the rooms in the house, several times over the years. She was still painting and wall-papering when we moved into Barnes Street.

Social Life
We had a busy social life during our first years on Parira. A house warming was held in the woolshed on 4 January 1946. Alister and Margaret had helped to get the shed ready on the previous day and the YFC helped to organise the evening. At supper time, Eric Hall held a cream sponge out to Ellen. When she took a piece, it was not cut through and the plate pulled out of his hand. The plate dropped on the floor and Eric got cream all down his trousers.

We attended the weddings of Mary and Bob, and Lloyd and Margaret. We drove to the latter in Mrs Cleland's car. In June, Ellen's mother left Newburgh to move into Timaru. We attended her clearing sale and a couple of days later her farewell.

Several of Ellen's friends and sisters came to stay: Sheila Deihl, Joyce Buckley, Miss Price, Auntie Nell and Olive. Jessie stayed for a week, and Ellen's mother also came and stayed a week. Mary came and stayed the following year. Thelma also stayed for a few days. Jessie and her friend Edna came to stay for a few days again in 1951

According to my diary for 1946, we visited someone around the district or further afield on most Sundays: Howells, Wiselys,

Donald Burnett, Viv and Sadie, Peg and Evan, Squires, Mr Gainsford (his wife had died), Gillinghams, Noel Kingston. Some of the people who visited were Mrs Lamb and Mrs Crawford, Lloyd and Margaret, Mr and Mrs Byrom, Harry Wisely, Mr & Mrs RG Cleland (Uncle Bob), Mrs Malthus, Eddie Kelynack. Jim Calder came for tea several times.

We attended a number of dances and balls in Cave. I was the Master of Ceremonies for the YFC ball. For a fancy-dress ball, we dressed as Mr and Mrs. We went to an Abbot and Costello movie called Rita Rio in Timaru.

The Farm was the venue for several events. In 1948, Hedley Squires came and "showed pictures" in the woolshed at night on the first slide projector in the district. The YFC held their dog trials on Parira and Ellen hosted the Women's Division.

In August 1948, we went to a concert at night after being to a field day. The next year, we went to the Plunket Society ball (Ellen was secretary) while Gran looked after Alan and Ronald. In December 1952, we also went to see a circus at night, but the diary does not say if the boys went. We also saw Brigadoon that year.

At the beginning of July 1952, we took the boys to see a movie about the coronation called "Elizabeth is Queen. The coronation had taken place a month earlier. With no television, we had to wait to see important events. The entire Cannington School went into Timaru one afternoon in 1960 to see a film of highlights of the Rome Olympics. In January 1954, the whole family went to see the Queen and Duke when they visited Timaru. They arrived on a train that stopped at Ashbury Park. Two days later, I took the boys to a circus at Anzac Square in Timaru.

In 1955, the whole family went to a church Garden party at Mt Nessing. That was the year that Dave Sewell left Cannington. I went to his clearing sale and the boys walked up to join me after school to get a ride home.

Sunday was also letter-writing day. If we were not out, Ellen would spend the afternoon writing letters. She wrote to her friend Sheila and Auntie Nell every week. She also wrote to any family members who were away from home. In addition, she had various other friends that she wrote to quite frequently. Sometimes she would have five letters ready to post on Monday. She did not just write a short note; as most of her letters were several pages long.

We always went to the Albury flower show. In 1947, Ellen won prizes for anemones, pansies, butter, rhubarb, tatting and crochet

Growing Family

In September 1946, I was concerned that the river might flood, so I took Ellen into Timaru to stay with her mother for a few days till the river went down. **Alan** Roderick was born three weeks later at 6 pm on 11 October 1946. He weighed 8 lbs 4 oz. Ellen stayed in hospital for two weeks. I was only able to visit three times, because I had no transport of my own. On a Sunday, Mum and I went in to visit, but we had trouble with the car and did not get there. Two days later I took it in for repairs. A few days later I went to town on the bus to visit. I had a meal with Ellen's mother.

The day after Alan came home, I was timekeeper for the dog trials at the Timaru show. When Alan was a month old, Ellen and I went to a concert. Gran looked after Alan to allow us to go out.

Alan had to go to the doctor several times for a problem with his eyes. In February he had penicillin put in his eyes and in May he went to see Dr Talbot.

In February 1948, while I was at church in the afternoon, Ellen had a miscarriage. I took her to the doctor, and then to stay with her mother. On Thursday, when I came to visit after going to the Holme Station sale, Ellen was still weak and in bed. I went to town and got her after going to church on the following Sunday.

On 18 April 1949, I took Ellen to Hospital at 4 am, but the baby was not born until 10.45 pm. I went to the Fairlie show and then to town to see Ellen at night. In those days, fathers were not allowed anywhere near the theatre. **Ronald** John weighed 10 lb 11 ozs. I went to visit three times before they arrived home a fortnight later. This was the normal time in hospital. For the first week, new mothers were not allowed out of bed. On 15 May, I was ordained as an elder at church. Gran looked after kiddies, so Ellen could go too. Henry Adam called at the end of May. Ronald was christened on 5 June. Ellen's mother and Jess came out for the day.

In September 1949, Alan and Ronald had whooping cough. For Christmas that year I brought down a pony for Alan. He did not really take to riding. I think that Stewart inherited all my horse skills.

On 22 October 1951, Ellen and I went to town at night to be with Jess, because the river appeared to be rising. The next day, I went to the Point sale, while Ellen stayed at Auntie Nell's. Ellen went into hospital at night. The next day Aussie calved, and Ellen had a little daughter, called **Jillian** Ellen. I went in to see Ellen at night. I wrote in my diary that I was "absolutely thrilled". I went to town to get Ellen and the baby when she was twelve days old. The boys had stayed with Gran and Helen. Helen took the boys and their clothes back to Parira. Auntie Nell came to stay a few days later.

In May 1953 when Jill was small, Ellen went into hospital for an operation. Anna Smidt, a Women's Divison housekeeper, came and looked after the children while she was away. She became a good friend and we later went to her wedding. Ellen was in hospital for two weeks and recuperated with her mother for a third week. When she came home, Aunty Nell came to help her for a while.

The Oudemans had arrived to work on the farm, so Ellen invited them for a meal when she got home. Aunty Nell was shocked that Mrs Oudemans did nothing to help, even though Ellen was just out of hospital and had a small baby.

Jean Isabel was born on 22 October 1954. I went to see them at night and wrote in my diary that I was "overjoyed'.

Stewart Donald was born at 12.30 am on 6 July 1957. Betty Ross, a Women's Divison housekeeper, came to look after the children. They all thought that she was wonderful. Ellen and Stewart came home after 9 days in Jean Todd.

In October 1958, Ronald was in bed with measles. A week later Alan and Jill had them. In those days, the school had quarantine rules and children were not allowed to return to school until several days after the spots had disappeared. Once they felt better, it was like having extra school holidays.

A week before Christmas in 1958, Ellen had to go to the dentist with a painful tooth. She had to go again on Christmas Eve and have gum opened, cleaned out and stitched again. It was very painful.

In April 1959, Alan had to go to the doctor at night to get a fish bone out of his throat. We had fish for tea and he swallowed it by mistake. In May that year, Jill had her tonsils out. She was in hospital for four nights.

Alan started High School as a boarder at Thomas House in 1960. He took the Agriculture course, because he wanted to be a farmer.

Later that year, there was "great joy in our home", when Ellen gave birth to a baby boy called **Hamish** Peter. I went to town for Mrs Somerville, a Women's Division housekeeper. On the Sunday, I went to church and then to town to see Ellen in the afternoon. I took children to the park and Uncle Alex to the cemetery. Children were not allowed into Jean Todd, but they looked up towards the window of Ellen's room and she waved to them. Ten days later Ellen and baby came home and Mrs Somerville went home.

During 1961, all the children were vaccinated for Tetanus.

Telephone

When we moved onto Parira, the telephone was already there. We were on a party line and our number was 11R and our call signal was short-long-short. The telephone hung on the wall and had a handle to turn that rang the bell. When we wanted to talk to someone on our own line, we rang their code twice. For other local calls and toll calls, we would ring one long ring and the girl at the telephone exchange would connect us to the number we wanted. The exchange was an important source of employment for young women, as an operator was on duty every day from 7 am to 11 pm and 8 am to 8 pm on Sundays.

When we picked up the phone to make a call, we would say "working?". If someone was already using the line, they would answer yes. When we finished a call, we would give a short ring to let other people know that the line was free. There were five other families on our line: Crawfords, Riverbank, Hillview, our cottage and Wrights. This meant that getting onto the line could be quite difficult at times. Toll calls were very expensive, so we did not make many.

An automatic exchange was switched on in Cave on 1 December 1971. When it was introduced, we remained on party lines, but all the calling was automated.

Cars

In the early years, travel was difficult, as we did not own a vehicle. Sometimes we used Mum's car, but mostly we went to town on the bus. Even when a car was available, travel was not easy. Aunt Bessie died in January 1946. Uncle Jack, Uncle Bob and I drove down to Milton for her funeral, but we had a lot of trouble with the car, so we did not arrive until 8.45 pm. Uncle Bob and I stayed with Harry Wisely. We drove home after the funeral.

When I attended Dog Trials, A&P Shows, Field Days, Young Farmers Club, Farmers Union and stock sales, I usually got a ride with one of various neighbours: Mr Squire, Mr Campbell, Mr Blackmore or Uncle Bob Wisely.

In March 1948, we went to the Cannington homestead for the afternoon, but the car axle broke and it had to be towed home. A couple of days later we went to town and brought the car home after repairs. A few months later, I went to town to see Mr Marra about a car that he had been checking for me. I brought a Chev V8 for Mum from Reliable Car Sales for £422 plus the trade in for the old car.

We bought a Willys truck for £425 in March 1949, just before Ronald was born. The crop of grass seed on the Longridge Paddock yielded well, so we used some of the proceeds to buy it. We could only go out in the truck on a fine day, because the bassinet and pram had to go on the back. The Willys truck was our vehicle until October 1953, when we sold it and brought a 3-ton truck at Winchester. We got the upholstery on Gran's V8 fixed up and used it, until we bought a new Standard Vanguard in September 1955.

The Vanguard was not totally reliable. In 1959, I took it into town for repairs and brought Uncle Alex's car home. Two days later, I took Uncle Alex's car back to Timaru and brought ours home. I took Mum's hens into town to be sold at the same time. A year later in March, the car was back in for a couple of days to get a valve grind. This had to be done every one hundred thousand miles.

On one occasion when we got stuck in water by the Holme Station bridge, I had to roll up my trousers and get out of the car. I used the crank handle to turn the engine and get the car out of the water. Once the engine dried, it started again.

Holidays

In the early years on Parira, we managed to get away for several holidays. Ellen was away for a couple of days in November 1947, when she attended Joyce Buckley's wedding in Dunedin. Gran looked after Alan during her absence.

In May 1947, we spent nearly two weeks on holiday in Dunedin. On the way back, Ellen and Alan stopped at Oamaru to stay a couple of days with the Diehls. I went into Timaru to pick them when they returned on the train.

In May 1950, I had a hernia operation in Timaru hospital. Ellen came to visit me in the afternoon. The next afternoon, Gran and Ellen came to see me. Olive came to stay with Ellen for the weekend. On Monday, I was able to go home, so Ellen came in for me. At night Olive and Al went to a play at Cave. The next day, I spent some time mending Ronald's crawlers. While I was recuperating, I took Gran to see the movie "Gone with the Wind". A week later, the stitches were removed.

A week later, we went off on holiday, leaving Ronald and Alan with Gran and Helen. We stayed the first night with Lloyd and Margaret at Rokeby. The next day we went to Rakaia Gorge, calling on the Carrs and the Campians on the way. The next day, we sat in the sun, before going to see Jean Fyfe. We then went to Christchurch and stayed in the Federal Hotel. We visited Aunt Bell, who lived in Christchurch. On Sunday, we went to church and then went for a drive over the summit road. Monday and Tuesday were spent at the NZ Championship dog trials at Tai Tapu. We went to Margaret's at night.

On the way home the next day, we called to see Noel Kingston, who had farmed at Mawaro. We had been away for eight days. Gran said that Alan was quite excited when we arrived home. After afternoon tea, we packed all our goods in the truck and went off home.

Our 1951 holiday began as a bit of an ordeal. I went to the Point sale the day before we were due to leave. The Willys truck broke down, so I left it in Pleasant Point to be fixed. The next day we left Alan and Ronald with Gran and headed off for a holiday in Nelson. We stayed the first night with Margaret at Ruapuna. I spent the afternoon at a blacksmiths watching how he worked. I was worried because the truck was running very hot. In the morning we left for Christchurch, but stopped at Ashburton to have the truck fixed. We spent the night in Christchurch, where we went to the pictures.

The next day we left Christchurch for Blenheim, where we stayed at the Masonic Hotel. We stopped for lunch at Kaikoura. At night, we went to pictures again. The next day we had a shock absorber repaired on the truck before going on to Picton. We stayed at the Terminus Hotel. The next day we went to Nelson via the Grove Road. We stayed at the Metropolitan Hotel for four nights. On Saturday night we went to pictures and on Sunday we went to church twice. We went for a drive to Takaka and saw the largest spring in the world and visited a cement works. On the way home, we stayed at The Lodge in Hanmer, where it snowed overnight. When driving towards Christchurch, we ran into heavy rain. We stayed a night at the Federal Hotel and went to the pictures again. On the way home, we had lunch with Lloyd and Margaret.

Gran noted in her diary that the frosts had been very cold. "Alister put the fire on at Ellen's ready for them coming home, but the pipes were all frozen, so he had to let the fire go out. Ellen and Rod got here shortly after 4 pm. Alan and Ronald went home with them. We had to put on a fire in the sitting room to warm up the house". The pipes thawed out the next day.

Changes to the House

Mr Kenton came to do up the boy's room in 1957. He lined the walls with Pinex wallboard and put Feltex on the floor. That winter, we pulled out the Macrocarpa hedge by the garden and put in a new netting fence with wooden rails. This let much more sun into the boys' bedroom.

In February 1959 we put a new Atlas stove into the kitchenette. It cost £61-7-6. Mr Kenton painted the living room. The next year, he did up our bedroom.

Mr Kenton came out again in 1961 and painted the house. It took nearly a month. The walls were painted a blue/green colour and the roof orange. Ellen got frustrated with Mr Kenton because he smashed down a lot of her plants.

Many changes were made to the house over the years. During August 1963, Mr Esler came out and lined boy's bedroom at the front of the house. Alan had left school by then, so he assisted Mr Esler. When they were finished, Ellen and Ronald did the wall-papering.

Lester Hill cut down the large Lawsoniana tree at the back of the house and Alan dragged the branches away with the tractor. The old wood shed was demolished as well. A new fence made out of corrugated iron was built at the back of the house.

Mr Esler came again to line the sitting room and girls' bedroom in 1965. I bought a new freezer for Ellen on our twenty-fifth anniversary. Ronald painted the roof of the house in charcoal. Jill helped to paint the walls white.

In 1967, Mr Esler came and put new roofing iron on the living room roof. He also put in a new terrace at the front of the house with double doors leading out from the lounge.

Mr Esler also put in a new path out to the front gate. We cut down the Marocapa hedge beside the garage and put up a new fence. The next year Mr Esler came and put in new wardrobes and cupboards in Jean and Jill's room and Alan and Ronald's room.

In 1969, several changes were made. Ronald and Ellen papered and painted the living room. Mr Esler came and lined the bathroom and put a shower in the back of the pantry. This reduced the size of the pantry, but it was great to have a shower. Ellen and Ronald painted the bathroom when Mr Esler was finished.

In 1969 we bought home a new settee for the living room. The following year we bought a new table and chairs for the living room after we had papered and painted it.

In 1975, we had a new skyline garage built for $1052.30. Fraser Esler also came and built a freezer room in the wash house. He did a really good job and was pleasant to have around. Ellen painted both rooms when he had finished. She also painted and papered the girl's room.

Managing the Household
(Ron)

Well Organised

Mum ran a well-organised household working to a regular routine. Monday was wash day. All the family would put on clean school clothes and old clothes for around home. All the clothes that had been worn the previous week would be washed and hung out to dry. Later in the day, they would be brought in and ironed and put away in the drawers. The ironing was done on the end of the living room table. Mum put a blanket down on the table with a sheet for an ironing surface.

The sheets were washed on Friday. Mum made all the beds every day. We always had three sheets on our beds, with one above the blankets beneath the bedspread. On Friday, the bottom sheet would be removed for washing, and the other two would be moved down. A clean sheet would be put on the top. All the dirty sheets would be washed and hung out to dry on a long clothesline in the yard. When the washing was brought in at the end of the day, one of the children would help fold the sheets before they were ironed. They would then go into the cylinder cupboard for airing, ready to go back onto a bed the following week.

When the sheets became too badly worn, they would be cut in half down the middle. Mum would sew the two outside edges together and hem the outside. This would make the sheets last a little longer.

When she was a little girl, Mum had been called Mrs Polish. She never really escaped from cleaning shoes. On Saturday afternoon, she would get out the good shoes for all the family and clean them. We were responsible for cleaning our shoes for school, but Mum would have them shining ready for church on Sunday. This made us a bit lazy, as we would try to make that one clean last for a week.

One day a week, Mum would polish the linoleum floor in the living room and kitchenette. Dad bought an electric polisher, but Mum did not really like it. She preferred to get down on her knees and rub the wax polish on with one cloth and wipe it off with another. On other days she would just mop the floor with a mop.

In October, when the men were busy tailing lambs and the norwest winds were blowing, Mum would spring clean the entire house, one room a day. All the furniture would be moved and the floors vacuumed, the woodwork would be washed and the drawers cleaned and tidied. The curtains would be taken down and washed. The blankets on the beds and the bedspreads would also be washed too. Each room would be spotless when she had finished. The last room to be done was the kitchenette. Mum would empty each cupboard and wash it completely, before packing everything away again.

Sewing and Knitting

When Mum was first married, she bought a second hand Singer sewing machine. She was delighted when she was able to buy a new Elna sewing machine that used disks to make fancy stitches. It also went backwards and forwards and made buttonholes. Mum made almost all the dresses that Jill and Jean wore. When they went to boarding school, they needed about five dresses, so Mum made them all. When Jean went to training college, she was kitted out with clothes made by Mum.

The sewing machine was also used for mending clothes. Mum would patch any holes in our working trousers and shirts. Sometimes she turned the collars on shirts that had worn out. Even in the evenings, she never relaxed. She would sit in a chair and darn socks that had holes or get out her knitting. Each member of the family would have a jersey or cardigan knitted for them.

Meals

Feeding a hungry family was a demanding task. We grew up towards the end of the time when farming was hard physical work, so we ate big meals, including a cooked breakfast. During the winter, this would be porridge followed by bacon, sausages and fried eggs, saveloys and poached eggs, or scrambled eggs. On Sunday morning, we had a boiled egg in an egg cup. During the summer stewed fruit and Kornies replaced the porridge.

We normally had a cooked lunch, but the main meal was dinner at night. This usually consisted of meat, potatoes and two vegetables and would be followed by a dessert. On Sunday, we always had a big roast dinner after church.

If Dad was working close to the house, he would come in for morning and afternoon tea. Mum would always put out something buttered (scones, loaf, muffins, sugar buns or bran biscuits) and two different types of cake or biscuit. When we arrived home from school, we would be given a couple of bits of cake for afternoon tea. We were not allowed to eat anything until we had changed into our old clothes. If Mum was away, she would leave two cake tins on the bench. Each of us would take one piece from each tin. We would never take more than one piece of each or go into the other tins, even when she was away.

Mum was a good cook, but keeping the tins full was a big job. On baking day, she would work for most of the morning, baking several different items to make the most of the hot oven.

Meals were always quite formal. At about 4.30 pm, after the dinner was prepared, Mum would go and "get tidied". She would change out of her work clothes into a better dress and do her hair ready for dinner.

The table was always set, and we always sat at the table, even for lunch and breakfast. The jam was put out in dishes with jam spoons. We were expected to take some butter with a butter knife and put it on the side of our plate, before putting it on the bread or toast.

Dad would sit at the head of the table. Two of the boys would sit on a form at the back of the table, and the girls would sit on the other side. For a tea meal, a loaf of bread would sit on the breadboard beside Dad. He would slice the bread and pass the slices around the table on the knife. Dad got upset when Mum cut the bread, as she tended to get the loaf crooked. For a while, we had a bread slicer with a circular blade and a handle to turn. It also sliced bacon. When it got blunt, Dad went back to using the bread knife.

After the evening meal, we would often gather around Dad at the end of the table for a couple of songs. The two younger children would sit on his knees and the others would stand around him. Dad would lead us in singing the songs he had enjoyed when he was a boy. We got to enjoy many old songs, like "The Stone Outside Dan Murphy's Door", "When Irish Eyes are Smiling", "Two Little Girls in Blue" and the "Mountains of Mourne." Dad also played a game called the Dusty Miller, which the younger children really enjoyed.

Dad loved to sing. As we drove home from Church, he would sing one of the hymns that we had sung that day. One of his favourites was "O God of Bethel by whose hand, thy children still are led". He also sang as he went about his work.

Garden

Mum grew enough vegetables to feed a large family. She had a systematic way of sowing out the garden, so that vegetables were always ready to eat. New lettuces would be planted every few weeks. Other vegetables were sown late in the season, so they would be ready to eat during the winter. The vegetable garden was large, but it was not large enough for Mum. Dad fenced off a small piece of the Cow Paddock to grow peas and potatoes. The fence opened up at the end, so it could be cultivated with the tractor and grubber, but once this was done, Mum did the rest of the work. Any surplus was packed into the freezer.

The garden also contained raspberries, strawberries, black currants and gooseberries. Mum picked them all and nothing ever went to waste. The orchard grew peaches, plums, pears and apples. Mum picked all the fruit and what could not be eaten was preserved or frozen for later use. The apples from the orchard were supplemented with others purchased from Butcher's Orchard at Fairview.

Each summer, Mum would preserve peaches and apricots that Dad purchased at Morton's Auction Rooms in Timaru. In 1973, she purchased 5 cases of apricots for $2.00 each and 5 cases of peaches for $1.90 each. The good fruit was preserved in glass jars, and the riper fruit would be made into jam.

Mum also kept a large flower garden. Flower beds extended along both sides and the front and of the house. The area at the front included a shrubbery, herbaceous border, formal rose garden and large lawn on which we children could play. Mum loved flowers and her garden was full of bright colours. She frequently won prizes at flower shows and competitions at Womens' Division.

Mum planned her garden, so there was colour all year round. She rarely went to a garden shop. Most of the plants were grown from seed or grew from cuttings that she got from other people's gardens. Others came from the bring-and-buy table at Women's Division, or by swapping with friends.

Walking in the garden was restful for my Mum. When her sisters or friends visited on a Sunday, she loved to take them around the garden to enjoy the colours. Each plant had a story. When her visitor commented about a plant, Mum would tell the story of how she obtained it and described the person who had given it to her.

Ducks and Geese

Mum kept Muscovy ducks in the orchard. One of the younger children would be responsible for feeding them with mash or scraps from the kitchen. That was in the days before frozen chickens were readily available, so we would eat duck when Mum wanted a treat for Sunday dinner.

When a batch of ducks was mature, Dad would kill them and all the children would help Mum to pluck their feathers. They had to be scalded in hot water to allow the feathers to come out. Plucking ducks was hard messy work and we soon got tired of it. Once the ducks were plucked, they had to be gutted to remove the innards. The dressed ducks would go into the freezer ready to be eaten. Later on, Mum kept Aylesbury ducks, because they were white and easier to pluck.

Dad kept a pair of geese and a gander out on the back facing of the Cliff Paddock. Sometimes they would nest and hatch out several goslings. When the young geese were fully grown, he would bring them into the sheep yards using a heading dog to control them. If they were fat, they would not be able to fly. The young geese would be killed and the older ones would be released to breed again.

Hens

Mum always kept about twenty hens to provide eggs for the family. When she arrived on the farm, Gran gave her some pullets. They went to town and got some chicks in September. They also got three broody hens from Mrs Oliver to keep them warm. In 1957, Uncle Jack built two new fowl houses, one for the hens and one for the pullets. He also built a small shed for raising the chicks.

When we were young, Mum would buy day-old chicks from Mrs Gosling at Pleasant Point. Dad had bought a kerosene brooder to keep them warm. If the brooder ran out of kerosene or got blown out by the wind, this was a real crisis, as the chicks would die, if they got too cold. Dad would check the brooder every night before going to bed. After about three weeks, the chicks would have enough feathers to keep warm without heating. They were fed mash and crushed grain.

The chicks grew into pullets in a few months and would start laying in the new year. When the older hens finished laying in the autumn, they would be taken to the CCD and sold. The pullets would be moved into the hen house, and the pullet house would be cleaned out for the next lot of chicks to move into.

Dad would let the hens out in the morning. At night one of the children would go out and throw some wheat into the hen house. When all the hens had gone in, the door would be shut for the night

The child who fed the hens would collect the eggs at the same time. When eggs were plentiful, some would be preserved in a big drum in the pantry. These would be used for cooking during the winter, when eggs were scarce.

The hens ate mash from big feeders. One of the boys would get a big bucket of mash from the feed house, and carry it over to the hens. They would also get straw to line the nests and for litter on the floor of the hen house.

One task during the winter was to clean out the floor of the henhouse. Alan and I would load the manure onto wheelbarrows and carry it into the garden. Mum would only allow threshed straw to go into the hen house, so that the manure would not grow weeds.

Rats were always a problem around the hens. They would dig holes and nest under the concrete floor in the workshop next door. One time when we were cleaning out the hen house, we opened up some rat holes. Alan speared one with a fork and I killed the other with a shovel. Great excitement!

Mum got really upset if a hen got into the vegetable garden. All the children would be called out to chase it from the garden, before any of the vegetables were damaged. The only thing worse was for someone to leave the gate to the cowshed open. A couple of times a cow got in and started feeding on the cabbages. A cow could do a lot of damage very quickly, so leaving the gate open was a serious crime.

In 1969, Dad moved a fowl house from Hillview and put it out at the back of the cow paddock. This allowed the hens to be more free-range, which improved the quality of the eggs, while reducing their feed requirements.

Pigs

Dad often kept a pig to feed on the surplus skim milk. The pig was also fed barley soaked in water and scraps from the house. Every pig that he reared seemed to be called Snoot. In the early days, Dad and Uncle Alister would kill and dress the pig themselves. Dad would shoot the pig with a 0.22 rifle and Uncle Alister would stick it with a knife to allow the blood to drain out. The pig would then be put in a trough of hot water and scraped with a garden hoe to remove the hair. The boiling water would have been heated in a copper. Sometimes they would cure the bacon themselves, by soaking the chunks of meat in brine for a couple of weeks and then hanging them to drain.

Later on, Dad took the pig to the abattoirs to be killed. Fairbrother's Butchery would roll the meat and make it into bacon and ham. This was much easier than making bacon on the farm.

Meat

About once a fortnight, Dad would kill a sheep for the house. He would keep the sheep in the woolshed overnight, so that its stomach would be empty. We enjoyed going out to watch, but he made us wait outside until after the sheep's throat had been cut. When the sheep was dead, Dad would open the door for his helpers to join him. The first task was to tie a knot in the gullet, so that the stomach would not leak. Then he skinned around the legs and down the brisket.

A gambrel would be attached to the hind legs and the sheep would be hoisted up on a block and tackle with some of the children swinging on the rope. The remainder of the skin would be pulled from the back of the sheep and hung on the fence to dry. The skins would later be taken to Timaru and sold.

The most exciting part was when the sheep was cut open to remove the offal. The stomach and intestine would be removed first. While it was still warm, food could be squeezed around the intestine. The next step was to remove the heart, lungs and liver. Dad would sometimes cut open the heart, so we could see the various chambers of the heart. The lungs were bright pink and if cut open the air passages inside were visible. The liver was dark brown. If the sheep was young, Dad would remove the gall bladder and take the liver into the house to be cooked with bacon. Sometimes, he would crack open the skull so we could see the brain.

The lower legs were removed, because there was no meat on them. Dad showed us how to poke into the knuckle and grab a sinew. If you pulled hard on it, the hooves would bend up. All this activity gave us a good knowledge of anatomy.

The carcass would hang overnight, wrapped in a muslin bag to keep out the flies. The next day, Dad would cut it up into roasts and chops. The dressed meat would then be hung in the meat safe behind the washhouse. One of us children would sometimes be sent out to the safe to get some meat. Leaving the meat safe door open was the worst crime that could be committed. If a fly got into the safe, an entire carcass could be flyblown. If it was not too bad, the fly struck area would be cut off, so that the meat was not wasted.

Dad would take the offal to an old copper beside the hen houses and cook it up, so that it could be safely fed to the dogs. The copper was stoked with wood from a heap of old fence posts. Cooking was necessary to prevent the spread of hydatids, which had been a serious disease in New Zealand. If he had killed a sheep for dog tucker at the same time, there would be two lots of offal to cook up.

We mostly ate mutton, but Dad would sometimes send a cattle beast to the abattoir and get it cut up by a butcher. Mum would pack the meat into the freezer. The beef was a welcome change from mutton.

Going to Town

We generally went to town once during the school holidays to purchase new clothes or shoes for the next school term. We would set out about 9.30 am to arrive in town early. Dad would park the car at the Farmers Garage in Beswick St, and we would go over to the CFCA. Mum bought most of the clothes that Alan and I wore in the menswear department. She knew the names of all the men who worked there and would inquire about their families. When she had bought some parcels, we would take them back to the garage across the street. The cars were parked upstairs, but there was a shelf downstairs where we could leave our parcels. We never feared losing them.

After Mum had bought the clothes that Alan and I needed, we would walk down Stafford St to Cliff Brooks to get our haircut. When he had finished cutting our hair, he would give us a choice of Brylcreem or Bay Rum. We always chose the Bay Rum, because we had Brylcreem at home. When we paid for the haircuts, he would give us each a packet of Wrigley's chewing gum. We always chose Juicy Fruit. When the family grew up, Dad bought some clippers and cut all our hair.

At lunch time, we would meet at the Beverly Tearooms for a meal. My favourite dish was savoury sausages. In the afternoon, Mum would go to the butcher and Lurajud's fish shop to buy fresh sausages and fish. She would often go to Mays bakery and get fresh buns for tea. By the time we got home, we were all very tired, but

Mum always cooked something while Dad did his chores. We never ate takeaways.

New Cars

At the beginning of 1961, Dad brought home a new car, an Austin Westminster A99. Back then it was almost impossible to by a new car due to import restrictions. Dad had put his name down on the list with a new car dealer, but the names would hardly move. There were rumours of people paying money under the table to get their name to the top. A few lucky people had overseas funds and were able to buy a new car.

One day when Dad was in the Farmers Garage, they had a black Austin for sale. The lower half had been painted lemon/green for a client, who did not like it when he saw it. They said Dad could buy the car, if he didn't mind the colour. This was the only way he could get a new car, so he bought it. Our car was very distinctive round South Canterbury, with its lemon/green and black colour scheme.

The A99 had overdrive, so it would cruise along really nicely. There was an arm-rest in the middle of both the front and the back seats that one of the little children could sit on. These days it would be considered a dangerous practice, but the little children loved sitting up where they could see. In February 1969, the clutch of the car went, and Dad had to leave it at the garage to be repaired. He drove it in without a clutch, after starting it in gear and doing a kangaroo-hop start.

Dad traded the Westminster for a new Gold Austin 1800 in May 1969. This lasted until June 1974, when he bought new Austin Maxi in a colour called Olive-a-Twist. In 1984, Dad bought a Datsun Sunny Car with 13,000 km for $11,900 with a $6,200 trade-in for the Datsun Station Wagon they had bought some years earlier.

Childhood Fun
(Ron)

Parira was a place with plenty of things for children to do. At the back of the house was an area of trees bounded by a loop of the creek and the boundary fence that we called "The Jungle". Alan and I spent a lot of time down there building roads. We built a road that went from the house, down through the creek, across the jungle, back through the creek on the other side and up a cutting to the back of the cow shed. We spent many hours digging out the cutting up the steep bank.

The most challenging task was building a bridge over the creek. The creek dried up during the summer, but was a steady stream during the winter. When Mum had the alterations done to the lounge, a hole was cut in the weatherboards for a new door. We took the old weather boards and the hardwood studs that had been removed from the wall and made them into a bridge. (I remember Dad being upset because we used lead-headed nails to nail the planks onto the bridge). We built piles out of old pieces of concrete path, and built an approach at each end out of soil. The bridge was strong enough for us to drive our carts across.

When the creek flooded the bridge would get washed away. We tied wires from the bridge to a couple of trees, so it would float on top of the flood and not get swept down the creek. After a flood, we would have a busy few days repairing the bridge and the damage to our roads.

Carts

Alan and I always had carts to play with. I got mine for Christmas when I was four. Dad had built it for me himself. He had made the front axle out of wrought iron, by bending it in the forge. The back was a brightly painted box, red on the outside and cream on the inside, with paint left over from painting the house. Later Dad built Alan a trailer to go behind his cart. It had a crane that Dad had made out of steel. It could be used to lift things and move them around.

Alan and I constantly rebuilt our carts (we called them our trucks). We used the axles and wheels as the base for various models. The best model had a flat deck with a steering tiller that came up on an angle allowing us to kneel on the cart and push it along with one foot. We got very good at driving and could go really fast around the paths and tracks.

Out in the sheep yards, there was a steep little hill. We spent many hours riding our carts down the hill and doing a "wheelie" at the bottom. Later we would go out into Eric's Paddock and ride down the hill there. The ride down was really exhilarating, but pushing the cart back up was really hard work.

Outdoor Fun

At the end of the winter, the empty hay barn was a great place to play. We would use the remaining hay bales to build houses or make tunnels into the stacks of hay. The woolshed was another great place to play on a wet day. We spent many hours playing hide and seek among the bales and in the fadges of wool.

The big Macrocarpa tree by the cowshed was another great place to play. We had hammocks, all types of swings, and a climbing rope hanging from the trees. We would have a circus in which each member of the family would have a turn at doing something daring.

The Cliffs were always fun. We would trek from one end to the other, walking along the sheep tracks.

Dad fed out a lot of hay, so there were always large bundles of twine available for our play. We learnt quite young how to plait any ropes that we needed from twine. By grafting in new pieces, we could plait ropes as long as we needed them to be.

River

During the summer holidays, we would spend every afternoon at the river. There were several deeper holes over the road from the house that were good for swimming. When we got tired of swimming, we would lie in the shade of the willow trees, build dams in the river, or fish for cockabillies using a toetoe with a slip knot on the end.

One summer, we found a huge plank that had been washed down by a flood. We spent several days dragging it across the boulders and floating it in the water where possible to make the load lighter. When we got it to our swimming hole, we nailed it onto a willow tree to use as a diving board. It was not very springy, but it made a great platform to jump or dive off.

Another summer, we made rafts out of willow sticks. They did not provide enough flotation, so we tied a square kerosene tin to one end. Our paddles were a flat piece of wood with a handle nailed to it.

The river was full of toetoes. These were great for making arrows. We would put a small nail or piece of wire in the end to help them balance. We would make bows out of a piece of willow.

Indoor Games

On cold days we often played cards. Happy Family and Snap were the favourites when we were young. As we got older, we played Five Hundred, Sevens, Last Card and Cheat. I don't think Mum was very happy about that last one. We also played Funworder (a form of scrabble) and Monopoly. Jean remembers that she always wanted the dog for her marker, when we played monopoly, but Alan always got it. Ron always had the car and Jill had the shoe. So, Jean always ended up with the top hat or the iron.

Meccano was a popular indoor toy. Alan got a set for one of his birthdays, and it was added to with later presents. We always seemed to be short of nuts and bolts and wheels, but had great fun building all kinds of machinery. Later, Alan got a wind-up motor that could be used to make toys that moved.

Cotton reel tractors were fun for racing. A rubber band through the cotton reel was wound up on a stick. A piece of a wax candle was used to ensure it unwound slowly. The tractor would crawl along the floor, as the rubber band unwound.

Books and Songs

Books were an important part of our lives. Every child got a book at the school break-up and another at the Sunday School break up. We often got books for our birthday and Christmas presents. When Alan and Ron were young, Gran would give the next book in the Noddy series as a present. In this way, we built up the full series.

Before the youngest children went to bed, Mum would read a story to the entire family from her Ergermeiers Bible Story Book. When she reached the end of the book, she would start at the first story again. We enjoyed listening and gained a good knowledge of Bible history.

Dad was good at telling stories. He loved to tell us about life when he was young. He also told stories that he made up himself. When Mr Hay was the minister, he had a little Scots Terrier dog. Dad made up a whole series of stories about the adventures of this little dog when Jean was a little girl. I presume he thought about them during the day, ready to entertain us at night.

Entertainment

Life in the country was never dull, and our family took every opportunity to get out and about.

In 1956, a centennial procession was held at Winchester. Dad took the Sunday School children to watch it. In February 1959, the family went to see a floral procession through Timaru.

In October 1958, Dad took us to a traction engine rally at Tinwald. This was a great event. We saw two traction engines balanced on a see-saw and watched a mill threshing grain.

One year the school committee cut down some trees and pushed some of the old branches up into a heap. On Guy Fawkes night, the whole district turned up and we had a great bonfire. People let off fireworks and everyone had a great time. The fire smouldered afterwards for several days. We would take potatoes to school and cook them in the ashes for our lunch.

In February that year, we went into Caledonian Park for a fireworks display. There had been rain through the day, so the display was not as good as expected.

In June 1961, we went for a tramp up the Upper Pareora gorge on a Sunday afternoon. We drove up to Lindisfarne and followed the walking track up to the intake for the Timaru water supply. In several places, we had to walk on the pipeline to cross the river, which was a bit nerve-wracking. We did the same walk again the following year. On another occasion, we walked up to the waterfall on Nimrod. We climbed up beside the waterfall (a steep climb) and then up to the top of the bush-line and then came down a different way. Dad knew this area well from his mustering days.

We always went to see the circus when it came to town. The best circus was Bullens.

Movies and Television
During the late 1950s and early 1960s, Dad often took us to town in the evening to see a movie. I remember watching Polyanna, Greyfriars Bobby and one about a boy who ran away to join a circus.

During the early 1960s, someone started showing a film each week in the Cave Hall. We went to these quite often. These weekly movies at Cave were killed off by television when it became popular.

By 1964, television was coming into the district. The people of Albury paid to put in a repeater station on the Brothers, so they could watch the 1964 Olympic Games. A television was set up on the stage of the Albury Hall. I remember going there to watch the Olympics one night. Dad and Mum went to Jim France's to watch on their TV.

When Hamish and Diana McPherson moved into Riverbank house, they had a television. Alan and I would sometimes go up there to watch popular programmes. The picture was awful, and they would hang blue cellophane over the screen to block out the snow. Television was only black and white in those days. We got our first television at Parira in 1966.

Visiting Cousins

At various times, some of our cousins would come to stay. I think we were a popular holiday place. In the summer of 1955, Ferguson and Marguerite came to stay for a week. They really enjoyed swimming in the river. Alan and I went to stay with them, but we found the city boring. We went down to the carnival at the Bay each day, but otherwise, there was nothing to do and we were glad to get home again.

Alison and Claire spent a week with us in May 1961. They were both scared of Dad. I think their parents had told them he would teach them to behave well.

Aunt Shirley and Uncle Alister brought Margaret and Barbara up to stay for a week in January 1967. Hamish and Stewart went and stayed with them. Denise and John Waters stayed a week later in the year.

New Year's Day

New Year's day was always a holiday for the McKenzies. In the late fifties, everyone went to Caroline Bay for a picnic with some of the Cleland family. Dad's family would be there too. Uncle Alister and Dad would attend the Caledonian sports in the evening. The last time we went to the Bay was in 1957. The next year was wet, so we did not do anything. In 1959, the family went for a drive up to Lake Ohau and then on to Waitaki and home through Waimate. Uncle Jack came too. The following year we had a picnic at Waihi Gorge, while in 1962 we repeated the trip to Lakes Pukaki and Tekapo. In 1963, it was hot and dry, so we spent the day baling and carting hay.

The following year we went back to the Mackenzie country to see the Benmore hydro scheme being built. We drove up past Tekapo and back through Waimate. We went back again the following year.

We went to Temuka for a McKenzie family picnic in 1966. The next year, we had a picnic at Geraldine domain with Dad's family. The following year, we had hay to bale. Dad turned the hay in the morning before we went to a family picnic at Temuka. Alan came home early and baled 357 bales of hay. We carted the hay during the evening.

In 1969, Mum was staying with Jess at Auntie Nell's in New Plymouth, so the family did not go away. The next year, Dad, Mum, Jean, Hamish and Stewart went for a drive through Mackenzie Pass and up Haldon road to the top of Lake Benmore. They returned to Fairlie for New Year Procession. They returned to Timaru and had tea in gardens and then went to Caroline Bay to see the concert. The following year they did the same trip.

In 1972, Dad, Mum, Jean, Stewart and Hamish went to Peel Forest for a picnic. They had tea at Temuka, and the boys had a swim, before going on to Timaru to see the concert.

Christmas Day

Christmas was another family day. Our family spent the day with either Aunt Peg or Aunt Sadie through most of 40s and 50s. We would go up to Riverbank to meet with Dad's family in the evening. In 1954, we stayed at home, and the following year Aunt Olive and Uncle Len came for Christmas dinner. In 1957 we went to Aunt Sadie's, but we children did not enjoy it. From then on until the mid-1970s, we had Christmas day with Aunt Olive and Aunt Len. Sometimes, we went up to Burkes Pass, but mostly they came down to us. In 1969, Uncle Lloyd and Auntie Margaret were present as well.

Family Holidays

In May 1960, the whole family went for a holiday in Otago and Southland. We set out for Dunedin in the morning and arrived there at 4.30 pm, after calling to see Mum's friend Thelma at Oamaru. Going over the motorway was slow as the road was being rebuilt. The bed and breakfast hotel that we were supposed to be staying at had lost our booking, but they found somewhere else for us to stay.

The next day we carried on to Invercargill, running through showers on the way. We called to see Joyce Buckley in Green Island and Henry Adam at Milton. In the evening, we went to see Aunt Mary and Uncle Bob, as they were managing a motel in Invercargill. We stayed in a motel on Alice Street for five nights. On different days we visited Bluff and Mount Linton Station. One day we drove out to Dipton to see Mum's cousin after calling at a farm owned by Mr Calvert (a relative of Jan Hall). On Sunday we went to church morning and evening and drove to Fortrose in the afternoon.

Our next stop was at Alexandra, where we stayed in a holiday house that was only just finished on the Dunedin side of the river. We children had a great time playing among the large rocks and rushes. On different days, we went to Ranfurly to see the Dowse family and for a drive to Queenstown. We arrived home ten days after leaving, having enjoyed a rare holiday. We pulled a trailer all the way, which was a big load for the Vanguard.

In March 1966, Alan and I went on a holiday to Picton and Nelson, returning via the Lewis Pass. We travelled in the green Austin A40 and stayed in cabins at camping grounds. Margaret and Barbara stayed a weekend while we were away

In May 1966, Mum and Dad, Jill, Jean, Stewart and Hamish went on a ten-day holiday in Greymouth. Alan and I stayed at home and looked after the farm and I cooked the meals that Mum had prepared for us. They went over through Arthur's Pass and had tea with Aunt Sheila and Len after they had arrived at Greymouth

Motels. On different days, they went on drives to Lake Brunner, Franz Joseph and up the Hokitika River. They also went to Westport through the Buller Gorge and back to Greymouth down the coast. On Sunday they went to Church before having dinner with Sheila Diehl. They returned to Christchurch through the Lewis Pass and stayed three nights in a motel at Brighton. After driving through the tunnel to Lyttleton, they visited the airport and city before having tea with Margaret and Nort.

In June 1971 Dad and Mum had a holiday in Taranaki, where they stayed with Auntie Nell. Two years later, they had another holiday to the North Island, visiting Auntie Nell in New Plymouth and Uncle Jim in Auckland before visiting Tauranga, Rotorua, Napier.

In May 1972 Jean, Stewart, Hamish, Dad and Mum travelled to Te Anau and Invercargill.

Helping on the Farm
We all had chores to do every night. I would fill the wood box with wood from the woodshed and Alan would fill the coal bucket. I also remember cutting wood and kindling. We often helped Mum with the dishes. I remember periods when Mum would wash, I would dry the plates, Alan would dry the knives and forks and Jill would dry the pots and pans. At other times we would take turns at clearing the table and drying the dishes.

The boys were responsible for mowing the lawn. Alan and I would take turns or do half each. In 1960, Dad bought the first rotary mower making this chore easier.

Working with Stock
After school and during the holidays, we were often called upon to help Dad with stock work. The task that none of us really liked was drenching lambs. This was done in a narrow race beside the woolshed. It was just wide enough for two people. We would stand by Dad and push the lambs up tight. Once they were drenched, the lambs would be let back behind us. We would work up to the top of the race until the lambs had been drenched and the race was empty. It would then be filled up with the next lot of lambs. This was hot and dusty work, so we often took turns at helping.

We also helped Dad with crutching lambs. His back was stiff, so he would kneel and do the crutching. One of us would catch the lambs and drag them out to him. The other would sweep up the wool when he had finished each lamb and sort out the wool from the dags.

Dad would get us to drive the tractor or truck, while he was on the back feeding out hay.

Another frequent task was turning sheep in the gate when Dad was driving them up the road. (Jill says that she hated this task, as she was always scared that she would not be able to stop the sheep). The most difficult time was when the lambs had just been weaned. Someone would have to go down the road and turn the unruly flock in the gate to Eric's Paddock.

Lambing was always a busy time on the farm. One of our tasks was feeding the stray lambs that Dad brought in. Sometimes there could be a dozen to feed. On cold days, there might be a chilled lamb under a heat lamp that needed a feed, but they often struggled to drink.

In September 1959, Alan and Dad went to Holmes Station and brought home the ewes that he had bought. I went around the ewes at home while they were away. Earlier in the year, when there was a shortage of hay, the Cave transport bought a load of mangels for the milking cows. One of our jobs was to help feed them out to the cows. They were quite sweet to eat, if a piece was cut off with a knife.

Pet Sheep

Tiny was the first pet sheep that we kept. Mum had cared for her as a lamb. In 1955 she died and left us with a pet lamb. Alan had a pet sheep called Topsy and I had one called Rosy. Hamish had the best pet sheep. Dad had selected a well-bred twin lamb for him and she was fed well. She lived in the Cow Paddock and would come over to anyone who brought some sheep nuts. She mostly had twins or triplets, and one year she had quads.

Shearing

The whole family would be busy at shearing time. We would help Dad filling the pens with sheep and tramping down the wool in the wool press. The beginner's job was sweeping the board. You had to be alert, because you only had a few seconds between the fleece being picked off the floor, and the shearer arriving out with his next sheep. Sweeping the board made you feel really important at first, but the floor was hard on the feet and the day was long, so we soon learned that it was a fairly monotonous job.

We all looked forward to being promoted to picking up fleeces and throwing them onto the wool table, which was the next step up in the shearing shed hierarchy. We also learnt how to sew bales of wool and operate the wool press, but were not strong enough to pull it right down without the help of an adult.

The girls would often help with preparing morning and afternoon tea. Mum would make the tea in a billy and carry a basket of food out to the woolshed. The shearers would come into the house for their midday meal.

Fencing Turnips

A task that we did not enjoy so much was fencing turnips or young grass. Several of us would help with this task on a Saturday. Dad would drive the tractor across the paddock where we were putting up the break fence. One person would roll out the cyclone netting that had already been attached to a fence post. If the netting got caught up, it would fall off the back of the trailer and it would have to be lifted on again. Another family member would throw off a stake at regular intervals. Dad would dig a hole with a crowbar and hammer in the stake with a mall. While he strained up the netting with a wire strainer, we would staple the netting onto the stakes. Most of the stakes were hardwood, so this was difficult. Later on, we used tanalised pine stakes, which were lighter to carry and easy to staple.

The next week the process would be repeated. We would pull out the staples with fencing pliers, roll up the netting and load the stakes onto the trailer. Then we would put up a new fence. It all seemed a bit futile at the time, but I presume we were a real help to Dad when he was managing the farm on his own.

During the winter the sheep would be put onto a break of turnips or young grass for a couple of hours. One of the children would often walk or bike up to the paddock and open the gate to let the sheep on. They would all be waiting and would go through the gate with a great rush. A couple of hours later, we would go back with Dad to move them onto their run-off paddock again. Now they would not be so keen to move, so the assistance of a dog was required.

Docking Lambs

We often helped with tailing lambs. The first task was to set up the tailing yards in a corner of a paddock. In the earlier years, the pen for the lambs was made out of heavy wooden gates, with a larger pen built with stakes and netting to hold the ewes and lambs before the lambs were drafted. By the time we were helping, Dad had bought special yards build out of pipe gates. They joined together with hooks, so they were quicker to set up. The pen for the ewes was built with y-standard and scrim, with a long wing out one side to capture the sheep. The children would be spread out to ensure no lambs escaped around the end of the wing.

Once the lambs had been drafted off, we helped catch them. We felt good when we were big enough to hold the lambs while they were being tailed. They had their tails docked with rubber rings and received a vaccination against tetanus and pulpy kidney. The wether lambs were castrated with a rubber ring. Dad eventually bought a cradle to hold the lambs and make the process faster.

Bad Back

Dad was troubled for a long time with a bad back. The first reference in his diaries to being laid up was in 1950. He hurt his back carting hay and spent a few days in bed. The next year he was shearing at Campbell's, but had to stop on account of his back. Uncle Alister took his place. He went to town for an X-ray and was treated by Mr McKay. Next month he was back shearing Mr Robin's sheep.

In 1960, he was still going to town for treatment for his back. In July, when he finished crutching his back was giving trouble. However, the day after getting treatment, he was fencing grass for the ewes with the children helping him. He would be driving in the stakes, so he was not really resting. The next month, he had to go to town for treatment after shearing 120 ewes. He spent the night in town with Uncle Alex to have treatment again the following day. For almost two weeks during August, he was laid up in bed. He could not drive, so he depended on Uncle Alister, Aunt Shirley, Bill Wright or Mum for rides to town to get treatment. Mum had flu at the same time.

While Dad was in bed, I milked the cows before going to school, and fed the dogs and milked the cows at night. Alan was home for school holidays when the lambing started, so he was able to assist Dad. Jill had the measles, so because Alan had been in contact with her, he had to stay home from boarding school for an extra week. This was a great help to Dad.

Pneumonia

On 6 October 1961, Dad went to bed with flu. He went to the doctor four days later and was diagnosed with pneumonia, so he spent the next three weeks in bed. Uncle Alister did the general farm work and I did the cows and dogs, before and after school with Jill's help. The worst part was letting Cloud, who was very grumpy, off for a run each day.

On Labour day, Doctor Burnett and his wife and daughter drove out to see Rod. Uncle Alister got Frank Casey to come and help with the stock work. By the end of the month, Dad was feeling better, and on 4 November, he wrote in his diary that he was "poking about" again.

Cannington School
(Ron)

Starting School

Alan started school on 10 December 1951. I presume that he did not start on his birthday because Jill was born that month. He only had a few days at school that year, because the school picnic was held just four days later. Owen Latimer was the teacher. Alan had him as a teacher for two terms before Mr Gibson arrived.

Dad took Alan to school in the mornings and at night, he would start walking home, if no one was there to pick him up. One day Dad went up and could not find him. When he went back the second time, he discovered that he had missed Alan, because he had been walking on the bare patch of grass by the fence (where the sheep poked their heads through the fence and ate it clear).

Dad went to a school committee meeting at school to meet with the Education Board at the beginning of the next year, so he must have already been a member of the school committee. At the end of this year, the Gibson's came to visit for the afternoon, so Arthur must have started as teacher.

I started school on 1 February 1954. I was not five until April, but Mum believed in getting a good education and wanted me to have a head start. Garry Wright was starting in February and she thought it was best to start two pupils together.

Cannington was a sole-charge school when I started and Mr Gibson was the teacher. I don't remember much about my first days, but I can remember Mr Gibson making me a little notebook out of folded yellow paper. I was to write the new words that I learned in it. I was fascinated because the school had a stapler. At home, we always had to use a needle and thread to sew together the little booklets we made.

We learned to read from the Janet and John books. As we moved up through the series, we learnt more words. Getting to book 7 was a real achievement.

Teachers

Mr Gibson was my only teacher at primary school. I doubt that he was a great teacher, but I did learn a lot from him. He passed on some weird and interesting information. He taught us to enjoy poetry by reading aloud epic poems like the Inchcape Rock, Horatio on the Bridge and the How We bought the Good News from Ghent to Aix. His favourite line was from John Masefield's poem about Reynard the Fox,

> The fox was strong, he was full of running,
> He could run for an hour and then be cunning.

He also liked to read us nonsense poetry.

Mr Gibson was quite bad tempered and could "blow his top" if something upset him. We learned that it was better not to provoke him. He kept a strap in his drawer but rarely used it. I never got it, but I do remember Ted Haar getting the strap for peeing on the grass where the girls could see him.

The girls must have hated Mr Gibson because he was very hard on them. Some of them would get upset and lay their heads on their desks and sulk for hours. He said they had "gone into their shells" like snails. Some of the girls cried so much that the varnish on the top of the desk was damaged.

I felt sorry for the Gibson children having their father as their teacher. He was particularly hard on Andrew, his middle son. One day he was upset about Andrew's desk being untidy, so he took out his books and threw a heap into each corner of the room and told him to tidy them up.

School Room

When we arrived at school, we would hang our school bags in the porch. Every pupil had a leather school bag that hung on a shoulder strap. The boys would put the belt around our waist, and threw the bag over our heads and wear them like a backpack. The flap of the bag was held down by two buckles. We took out lunch in a metal lunch box. Once we had hung up our bags, we could head outside to play.

The school was heated with a pot belly stove that we called the Hot Dog. On a cold day, Mr Gibson stoked it with coal and coke until it glowed red hot and roared with a sound like thunder. Sometimes the gases inside would explode, blowing the lid with a loud bang and giving everyone a fright.

The little children sat on the south side nearest the heater, and as they progressed through the school, they moved over to the North side. The older children had big tandem desks with fold up seats and a shelf underneath for storing books, but I cannot remember where the little children sat. We had a long blackboard along the west side of the classroom, and each child had about a metre marked off, where they would practice their hand writing with chalk. When I was older and learning woodwork, we covered the blackboard with Pinex, so the wall could be used for displaying school work

The double desks were made out of kauri. When we got modern desks to replace them, the old kauri desks were taken outside and painted in bright colours. We would sit in them while we had lunch. I suppose they were eventually destroyed: such a waste of good kauri timber.

The school did not have a uniform, but the boys tended to wear grey cotton shorts and shirts.

School Routine

The school had a routine that continued most of the time that I was at primary school. At 9 am a bell would ring, and we would line up outside the school in two rows from oldest to youngest. When Mr Gibson gave the word, we would file into school.

The day often began with Morning Talks, when we talked about events in our lives. Then we would do Arithmetic for the next hour and a half. Once we were in the standards, there was an Arithmetic book for each year. I really enjoyed Arithmetic, and David Gray and I would work through the book together. We would do the exercises and get the Answer Book from Mr Gibson and check our work. We worked on our own, and Mr Gibson only had to help us if we came across something new that was hard to understand.

The whole school had to memorise the times tables, up to the twelve times. We would get tested on them frequently.

We would have a 15-minute break for Morning Play at 10.30. At the end of the break, Mr Gibson would ring the bell and we would return to our desks. We would then have to write down from memory in our spelling books, the three or five spelling words that we had been given to learn the day before. Those who did not get them right would have to write their words out several times, and do them again for the next day. For children who found spelling difficult, this was a real torment. While we were writing out words, Mr Gibson would write the words to be learnt for the next day on the board. We would copy them into our spelling notebook, to be taken home and learnt for the next day. Learning our spelling was our only homework

The spelling words came out of a book by a person called Schonell. The words were structured for each age group according to frequency of use and difficulty. When I was in about standard 4, Mr Gibson announced Schonell was out of date. Rather, we had to find words that we misspelt in our work, copy them into our spelling book and learn them. Spelling changed from being the great ordeal of the day to being rather casual.

After completing our spelling, we would get out our writing book. Each day we would be assigned a different letter of the alphabet to practice by writing out dozens of copies of this letter in a perfectly rounded form. The little children were only allowed to print. When printing reached a satisfactory standard, we were allowed to move onto writing. The younger children always wrote with pencils.

The next big milestone was using ink. Each desk had a hole at the front right-hand corner that contained an inkwell. Once a week, the ink monitors (older children) would gather all the inkwells and fill them up from the large ink bottle. We had to bring to school a wooden pen to which a nib was attached. A nib would last for about a month before getting twisted and becoming unusable. When writing, the nib had to be dipped into the ink after every two or three words.

Sometimes, when Federated Farmers or Young Farmers were using the school for their meetings, they would use the inkwells as ash trays. It was frustrating when you put your pen in and get a soggy mess.

Nibs that could hold enough ink to write a couple of sentences came available when I was in Form 1. I started using a fountain pen when I went to high school. Ballpoint pens were available, but they were considered to be bad for your writing.

The last hour of the morning would usually be spent writing on a set topic. Once we got our work completed, we were allowed to read. I learnt to write quickly, so I could get back to the reading that I enjoyed.

At midday, we would go out to lunch. We would have to sit still for the first twenty minutes, till the bell monitor had rung the bell and we could go and play, if we had finished eating our lunch. We developed the habit of eating our lunch quickly, so that we could go and play as soon as the bell rung. Sometimes Mr Gibson would check our lunchboxes to make sure that we had eaten out lunch.

After lunch, we would often listen to short programmes on the radio. Some were about social studies and literature. We also learned music over the radio. The radio choir conducted by Keith Newton would sing first, and we would sing after them. The boys did not enjoy singing that much, so we called him Chief Nuisance. Later Mrs Gibson taught us music. She played the piano which helped.

At the end of each day, we would put our chairs on our desks and gather all the rubbish. Ada Taylor had the contract for cleaning the school, so Mr Gibson made sure that we left it tidy for her.

School Books

During the first week of school, we would be issued with our new exercise books. Mr Gibson would put out a trestle table with a large roll of brown paper on it. We would cut paper off and use it to cover the books. We would fold it around the cover like an envelope.

A picture would be cut out of a magazine or Christmas card and glued onto the front to decorate them and make our books personal. When I got older, brighter coloured wallpapers had become more common, so we took wallpaper to school to cover our books, because it was brighter than brown paper.

Art

Every October the church had a flower show in Albury. For about three weeks before the show, we would spend the entire afternoon doing art. Each of us would put in several entries, mostly painting. We used powder paints for painting, but the colours were dull. The paint monitor would put powder in a glass container and stir in water. When I was older, the school got some poster paints. They were lovely colours to work with. I was not very good at art, so I never won any prizes.

Some of the older boys did linocuts. They would draw a picture on a square of lino and cut out the background. Once the cutting was finished, they put on Indian Ink with a roller, and try to print the picture on paper without smudging it.

The girls would enter flowers in the flower show as well. The little girls would put flowers in egg cups, while the older girls would decorate sand saucers.

Jill and Jean also entered embroidery and cooking that they had done at home. Mum gave a lot of help with the baking, so it was often as much her work as ours. On one occasion, she baked nine things in one day for show entries.

Woodwork

Dad had a workshop with tools and plenty of wood that we could use to make things. We were free to make and do whatever we liked. Later when Uncle Jack was at Hillview, we would go up and play in his workshop. He had worked as a carpenter, so had more tools than we had at home.

When Mr Ramage came to Cannington, he taught the older boys woodwork, because he had been a carpenter before he became a teacher. We built a workshop on the back of the shelter shed. Garry Wright and I built a Wendy House for the little children to play in. While the boys were doing woodwork, Mrs Gibson would teach sewing to the older girls. The younger members of my family went to Pleasant Point for manual training, but I never had that experience.

Getting to School

When I started school, Mr Gibson was picking up the children in his old brown car. I presume that he was paid to do this. He lived up the Cannington Road in a house that belonged to the McKerchars. He would travel down to school, picking up children on the way. After dropping the children off at school, he would travel down past our place and back round past Grays to pick up the rest of the children. The next year, he had a new blue Comer van which he used as a school bus. We called it the Cake Tin, because it was so square.

When the Baker children started school, Mr Gibson changed his route. He would go up Galway's Road, down the Motukaika Road and back over Martyn's Crossing to the school. I had to bike a mile down the road to Scott's corner to catch the bus. Alan was already biking directly to school. When Jill started school, I stopped biking and walked with Jill to catch the bus at Scots corner.

When I got a new bike for my birthday, I started biking to school with Alan. We rode a little over two miles, but the roads were shingle, so it was a tough ride. In the winter, we would have ridden about halfway to school, before the sun came up over "Braeval", so it would be very cold on a frosty day. We wore knitted gloves and a balaclava to keep warm.

We really hated the road being graded, because this made it hard to ride on. After a few days, the cars would form wheel tracks that were easier to ride on. The county council spreading new shingle on the road was even worse. The shingle crusher and traction engine often worked somewhere in the Pareora River. A bucket on a winch would drag the shingle up into the crusher. The crushed shingle fed into a huge hopper from which trucks could be filled.

We also hated days with a norwester in the morning and a southerly change at night. This meant we would have a headwind both ways. Riding home with a strong norwester behind us was great. We could get home without pedalling. When Alan went to High School, Jill joined me biking directly to school.

Swimming

During February, we would spend the afternoon swimming. When I started school, we did not have a swimming pool, so we would walk down to the river to swim. As soon as we had finished eating our lunch, we would start our trek to the river. We would walk down to the Cannington Bridge and then take a rough track through the gorse and broom to where the Pareora River joined the Whiterock Stream. There was usually a deep hole under the cliffs.

The older boys would find two clearings in the gorse, some distance apart. One would become the girls' changing room and the other would be the boys'. We would swim for about an hour and then get dressed and walk back to school. By the time we got back to school, it would be time to go home. We really enjoyed the swimming, but the long walk on a shingle road was hot and dry.

We were taught lifesaving using the Holger-Neilson method. The patient was laid down with hands under their head. Their back would be pressed to empty their lungs. Their elbows would be lifted up to fill their lungs. I don't know if the method ever saved lives and fortunately, I never had to use it. We also attempted to qualify for water skills certificates. It was hard to get reasonable distances because the swimming pool in the river was so short.

When I was about ten, a learners pool was built at the school near the front fence. We were glad to leave the long walk to the river behind.

School Environment
Along the front boundary of the school was a row of old pine trees. We would often play under them, making roads among the pine needles. We would also use pine needles and branches to build houses.

When I was in about standard four, the trees were felled. They lay on the ground for a few months before they were cut up and taken away. We had a great time building huts and forts among the fallen trees.

Outside the school was a rose garden. The long garden ran from the oak tree to the gate. We would each be given responsibility for a piece of this garden. Every second Friday afternoon, we would spend part of the afternoon weeding our plot.

Over by Cartwright's fence was a vegetable garden. The big boys would dig it up in the spring and sow vegetable seeds. They would tend it until school broke up. It felt like a waste of time because when we came back after the summer break, it would be full of weeds. I guess the school teacher ate the vegetables that ripened during the holidays.

The school owned about eight wooden-handled hand mowers. While the younger boys and the girls were gardening the big boys would mow the lawns. It was hard work on a hot day. During the summer holidays, there would be a roster for lawn mowing. Each week, two boys would bike to school and spend an afternoon mowing the lawns around the school room. We did not need to mow the upper playground as it had usually dried off and stopped growing.

The school often entered into a garden competition for the Hurdley Shield. In the weeks before judging, we would work hard on the gardens, but we never seemed to win the shield.

We were encouraged to have gardens at home. Packets of seed would be handed out to everyone in the spring. The girls were generally given flowers and the boys were given vegetables. We would work up a piece of ground in Mum's garden and plant the seed. In the autumn, the teacher and senior person from the district would come around and inspect the gardens. We were given horticulture certificates if our garden was up to scratch.

School Events

We used to go to the dental clinic at the Pleasant Point School twice a year. Most of the children hated going to the dental nurse, but our teeth were good, so we had no problems. The dental nurse gave us little dolls made out of cotton wool rolls, if we needed no fillings.

In October 1959, the school centennial was held. It started in the afternoon and was followed by a Banquet at night. Dad was on the organising committee.

At the beginning of 1959, a new schoolroom arrived. The pre-fabricated building was put in between the old classroom and the road. For the first year, Mrs Gibson taught the extra class. At the end of the year, Mr Ramage arrived to be the new teacher in the Junior School. He was also good at gymnastics. He built a vaulting horse and springboard and got us doing gymnastics for the first time.

124

Another memorable event that year was a visit to the Timaru Harbour that Dad organised through Uncle Jim, who was shipping manager for Dalgety's. We went on tour over the Gothic, a passenger ship used to bring migrants out to New Zealand. We also had a tour around the harbour in the pilot boat. This was very exciting for country kids.

School Games

One of the most popular games at school was hide and seek. The person who was "in" would have to close their eyes by the flag pole and count to one hundred. Most of us would hide behind the bike shed. When they came to look for us, we would all charge out at once. We had to get back to the flag pole and shout Home 1 2 3 before they could name someone they saw and call out Caught 1 2 3 while patting the flag pole. The odds were against them, as they would only be able to catch one person before the rest of the charging crowd got home. The fast runners would hide at the other end of the school behind the tank stand, because they could out-sprint the person who was in. Others would hide in the trees by Cartwright's fence. The first person caught would be "he" for the next game.

Marbles went through phases of popularity. We would play using a hole in a concrete path. We would start about four metres from the hole and take turns at shooting by flicking our marble with our thumbs. Once you got your marble into the hole, you took your turn from the edge of the hole and could shoot at the marbles of others before they got into the hole. If you managed to hit another person's marble, it became yours. The game ended, when every marble had either been shot into the hole or been hit by someone shooting from the hole.

We were not allowed to play "for keeps" and all the marbles were returned to their owners at the end of the game. David Gray had a marble-sized ball-bearing that he used. It was slightly heavier than a glass marble, so he won more games than anyone. We all envied him, but never changed the rules to exclude ball bearings.

The other popular games were Prisoner's Base and All Across. For Prisoner's Base, we would mark out a prison with a long rope. We would be divided into two teams; one in charge of the prison and the rest trying to get away. The prison guards would chase those on the outside and if one was tagged, they had to go into the prison. Anyone on the outside could let the prisoners escape, by putting their foot into the prison. They had to be careful they did not get caught, as the other side would have people guarding the prison.

We played All Across on the big field in front of the flagpole. Each child would choose a colour or a name of car or some other object. The person who was in would call the people across one at a time. The person in the middle would call out a colour and all those who had chosen that colour would have to run across without being tagged. Those tagged would have to join the person in the middle. If someone got across without being tagged, they would call out "All Across" and everyone would run and try to get across without being tagged. The secret was to think of an obscure colour, so you would only have to cross over with a group, and there was less chance of being caught (we trusted each other not to change the colour selected, if it was called). The game finished when the last person was tagged.

One summer the school was given a softball and bat, so we spent most of our lunchtime playing softball. We thought we were getting pretty good at softball, so we challenged the fathers to a game at the school break up. We thought we would be able to beat them, because they had not played softball before. However, the fathers were stronger and had good ball skills, so they beat us easily. So much for the confidence of youth.

Mr Ramage was English, so when he arrived, he got us playing cricket.

Sport

Once a year, we travelled to Pleasant Point for inter-school sports. We had to wear a white shirt with a blue C for Cannington sewn on the front. Later on, we went to combined sports with Springbrook and Southburn.

During the winter of 1959, Alan and I played rugby after Mr Gibson organised for the Cannington boys to play rugby on Saturday with the Old Boys Club. One of the parents would take us in as we

126

mostly played at Westend Park. Dad and Alister took Alan and me to watch the British Lions team playing South Canterbury in July that year. The Lions won the game 21 - 11

The older boys from the Cannington School went to see the French Rugby team play South Canterbury in 1961. All I can remember about the game is that when one of the French players rucked fairly vigorously, a lady ran out of the crowd and started whacking him with her umbrella. South Canterbury won the game. Alan and I went to Timaru again in June 1966 to watch the Lions play South Canterbury. They won the game 20-12.

About that time, Ray Leslie rejuvenated the Cave Hockey Club, so we all switched to playing hockey. Ray had played for New Zealand and was very keen. The school had bought some hockey sticks, so we spent most of the winter playing hockey on the tennis court. We quickly realized the benefit of an artificial pitch. On one occasion, we went to watch a touring Indian team playing South Canterbury. It was marvellous to see their skill.

We played hockey for Cave right through until we were young men. Alan was in the Cave senior team for several years. I only managed to make the senior reserve team.

Parira in the Sixties
(Ron)

Alan Comes Home

1962 brought a lot of change at Parira. Alan left school and came home to help on the farm. Dad was really pleased to have him, as since John Davies left in August the previous year, he had been managing the farm on his own. It was really too big for one person, so he was really glad to have the help.

In January, Margaret and Nort came down for the day. Jill and Jean went back with them for a holiday. Three days later Rod and Ellen had to go to Ruapuna for the girls, as Jill was homesick. Jill also started going to the speech clinic that year, as she had trouble saying her "w" sounds.

I started boarding at Thomas House in February 1962. I continued at Timaru Boys High School from 1962 to 1964. I did not really enjoy school, so I left at the end of the fifth form when I was fifteen (the leaving age).

1962 was also an eventful year for Stewart too. When Dad was cleaning out the sheds, he set a fire on the track to burn some old fertiliser bags. Stewart was walking backwards towards the henhouse, pulling his cart when he fell into the fire and burnt his leg. He went to the doctor twice to have it checked. A month later, he was in hospital to have his tonsils removed. He was in for four nights. Mum bought him a new blue dressing gown to wear in hospital.

Dad bought a pony called Tammy from Fred Howard for £40. Jill wanted a pony for Christmas, as some of her friends at school went to Pony Club at Baker's. She rode Tammy a couple of times, but quickly lost interest. I rode him around the sheep for a while, but he became redundant when we got a motorbike. Dad sold Tammy to the Cartwright's a few years later for £40.

In 1964, Mum had to go to the doctor with a sore leg. She was told to rest. When she went to the Fairlie show, a few days later, she sat all day in the car on account of her sore leg. A week later, she was out helping Dad feed the sheep.

1965

Another year of change came in 1965. Jill started as a boarder at Timaru Girls High School and I came also came home to work on the farm. Alan also went to Mt Cook Station and spent days helping Donald Burnett with mustering and shearing. This was the first of several trips. He also started spending quite a lot of time helping Hamish McPherson. In 1967 Alan was called up for military service. He spent three months doing military training at Burnham. He went back for a three-week annual camp during the following three years. When he returned from military service, Alan started working full time for Hamish McPherson. That year, he also bought his first car, a Morris Mini for $600.

In January 1965, Dad went down to Southburn to get a trailer load of old rams for dog tucker. A couple of them were stags (castrated as adults). We had been to a couple of rodeos, and all the way home Stewart talked about riding one of these sheep. When we pulled into Eric's Paddock to unload them, Dad held one while Stewart got on. He held on tight, but when the sheep tried to run, it eventually fell over. When they went to the doctor, Stewart had broken his collarbone.

Later that year, Alan went into town with Dad and brought home Grandma Cleland's old Austin A40 car. He bought it for us boys to use as it was very low mileage. When Alan bought his Mini, I had the exclusive use of the A40. It was not always reliable, but we mostly managed to keep it going. When I went to university, Dad used it as a farm vehicle. He took out the back seat and it would hold a couple of sheep. The boot lid folded down for the dogs to ride on.

More Family Change

As we grew older, our interests changed. For several years, we went to the Boxing Day Rodeo at Waimate. The first time was in 1964. We also went and watched Athletic Sports at Waimate a couple of times. There was a lot of interest in athletics after Peter Snell won his gold medals at the Olympics. All the top New Zealand athletes and some visitors from overseas would compete at Waimate.

Dad and Mum went to hear Jimmy Shand and his band play in Timaru. Mum and girls went to town to see a performance of Rose Marie.

In 1966, Mum spent a week in bed with a sore back and flu. This was unusual, as she did not get sick very often. The girls did the housework for her.

One Saturday during winter Alan, Ronald and Jill went ice skating at Tekapo with the Bible Class. David Hall caused a stir by driving his car off the road on the way back. He always said that he was avoiding a sheep, but I think he was paying too much attention to one of the girls travelling with him. On another occasion, the entire family went on a trip up to Mount Cook to see the mountains.

Jean went to a camp at Gunn's Bush. The next year she attended another with Mr Hudson at Lindisfarne. He was the man who took Bible in Schools at Cannington.

In January 1967, Jillian left by bus to stay at Lake Hayes with her friend Judy. She arrived back ten days later. Judy also came to stay with Jill several different times.

Grandma Cleland died early in the morning of 28 July 1967. She had lived on her own at Lisava Avenue. To a child, it always seemed to be a dark, cold house that we never enjoyed visiting. When Alan and I were at High School, we would sometimes go and have dinner with her. I remember having pineapple and ice cream for dessert and playing Monopoly with her afterwards. She was trying to be nice, but I felt like we never knew her very well. Her life had been hard and sad.

Dad brought the furniture out from Lisava Avenue and put in the woolshed. One Saturday afternoon, all Mum's sisters gathered together and took turns deciding what they wanted. There was a bit of disagreement about which order they should go in, but I presume most of the stuff was not of much value. Mum received $1273 from her mother's estate. She also received $2274 from her Father's estate, which was settled when the Lisava Avenue house was sold.

We had birthday tea for Alan's twenty-first birthday on 14 October 1967. John Coll and Aunt Shirley and Uncle Alister came down for the evening.

Stewart went to Aunt Olive's for a holiday in January 1968. Stewart and Hamish went and stayed at Uncle Alister and Aunt Shirley's that year as well.

Mum went with Jess to stay with Auntie Nell in New Plymouth during 1969

Seasons

The year 1961 began very wet and it was only with great difficulty that the winter feed was sown. The harvest was a real headache with a lot of grass seed spoilt with the rain. It remained wet right into winter and no ploughing was done. In July we had a big flood.

The weather came dry in the spring and by the end of the year, we had a drought. We had a big lambing, with nearly 2000 lambs from 1400 ewes. Dad had never seen so many twins and triplets before. He sold the lambs forward for 32/6 to Mr Scott from Kerrytown. In the summer we went down and picked plums on his farm.

1962 was a very wet year, but the lambing was very good. Alan stayed with lambing mob all the time on account of a big number of twins. The next year was just as wet, but the lambing was still good. Feeding the sheep became a problem on account of wet ground conditions. Dad got 1650 lambs away off the mothers, a good achievement.

In 1964, the farm got very dry through autumn, winter and spring. By May, the farm was the driest that Dad had ever seen it at this time of the year and he was feeding out hay. He started grazing sheep on the road. In June he brought home a trailer load of sheep nuts. He started feeding barley to some sheep. He sent the hoggets to Alister's new farm at Rosewill to graze on swedes and shifted the ewes to Riverbank.

The lambing was very good. By October the country was still very dry as there had been no rain of any amount since July. When Dad shifted the cows off the Riverbed, he had never seen so little feed in paddocks for cattle at the end of spring. However, the lambs did very well and he managed to get 1552 away off the mothers with an average weight of 30 lbs.

1969 was another very dry year. Dad and I trucked hoggets for feed at Riversdale in August. Millers Transport came with the first Mercedes Benz truck that we had ever seen. Dad sold some ewes to Clayton station. In November, he sold the cows with their calves for $108.00. He sold 660 lambs at a drought sale at Point for $4.55 a head. He sold another 800 to a farmer in Southland for $4.25. The drought broke with rain in December.

January 1970 was very cloudy with good rain. There was terrific growth, but by the beginning of March, the farm was dry again. The hoggets returned from Mr Bryant's place at Wendon Valley in

February 1970. However, it continued to be dry right through the winter.

In May, Dad and I drove a flock of 1000 ewes to grazing at Makikiki. We were very short of hay and I had calculated that this was the cheapest alternative feed, if we did not have to pay for transporting the sheep. The trip took three days each way. This was quite an adventure for me, because I had not really had a droving experience before. Jill and Alan fed the rest of the sheep while the drovers were away. A month later, we drove them back. When they returned, we fed them on grain. They did very well and we had an excellent lambing. A very mild winter with few frosts and an early spring followed, so there was plenty of hay in early summer, but by the end of the year, it was getting dry again.

Storms and Floods

In May 1961, the creeks and rivers were in flood. They flooded again in July following heavy rain. Our creek was the highest for four years and the river was the highest for 10 years. Dad and I put out hay for the sheep with the crawler tractor. The paddocks were very wet and Dad had never put hay on such wet ground. The rain lasted for two days, and most roads were blocked by the flood waters. The approaches to the Cliffs, Cannington and McKerchar's bridges were washed out.

Some of Uncle Alister's willows were washed out. Dad and I helped Uncle Alister to repair the damage to the fences. The children were off school for a week. For most of that time, we were without telephone and electricity.

The river and creeks flooded again in November the following year. Then in July 1963, there were three days of heavy rain, with five inches of rain altogether. Church was cancelled on account of the flood. Uncle Alister's farm was very badly damaged where the river broke in opposite both Campbells and Crawfords. Another flood occurred during January 1965. In May 1972, a large flood washed the Cliffs Bridge away. The old wooden bridge had to be replaced with one made of concrete. Martins Crossing was damaged badly in the same flood.

Dad watched the birds to understand the weather. A kingfisher would often sit on the power lines below the house. Sometimes he would call out with an urgent voice. Toot toot toot toot. Dad thought he was warning that a change was coming.

He also looked for the stilts returning to the riverbed as a sign that the spring was near. In later years, pied oystercatchers came to live on the farm. During the winter, wax eyes and fantails would often arrive when a storm was coming. They returned to the bush when spring and summer arrived.

Big Snow

In November 1967 the countryside was very dry. Most dams were empty and feed was very short. On 16 November rain started from the norwest at about 8 am and continued steadily through the morning. About 2 pm, it started to snow and by evening the country was covered with snow. Telephone and power lines broke and we were without power or telephone. The snow eased off by 10 pm, but by next morning it was snowing again. It snowed most of the morning. The snow was 5 to 6 inches deep at Parira. Albury had 14 inches, Fairlie 24 inches and Ashwick 5 feet. Crops everywhere were flattened and trees badly broken. Light rain kept on for most of the time, but seemed to have little effect on the snow. Alan and I put hay out to cattle. Dad went to town in the afternoon and took the stuff from the freezer to the Cool Stores in Timaru.

Two days later, most of the snow was gone. The creeks started to run with the melting snow and the river got high. The power was restored three days after the snow started. Mum and Dad went to Leo Neale and Shirley Watson's wedding at Albury, where there was still a lot of snow on the ground.

A few days later, Alan and I went snow-raking with Jim Campbell who had hoggets grazing at Ashwick Flat. This was a terrible job. The owner of the farm drove his bulldozer out to where the sheep were, making two tracks through the snow. We then had to get the hoggets onto these tracks. They were Romney hoggets, so they did not move easily. The day was hot, so the sweat

135

ran off your forehead down into your gumboots and froze. We were both badly snow burnt and our faces blistered.

Church and Community
(Ron)

School

Dad was the Chairman of the School Committee as long as members of our family were at Cannington School. Don Neale was the secretary for most of that time. Dad found him hard to deal with as he liked to keep things close to his chest. However, Dad kept the peace and the rest of the district thought they were a great team. The school committee met once a month. There were also various working bees to attend and involvement at the prize giving.

Arthur Gibson was head teacher most of the time that Dad was school committee chairman. He was single when he came to Cannington. After he had been in Cannington a year, he married Maree, a girl from Wellington. Dad told Hedley Squires that they would probably move to town, because she was not a country girl. Hedley said, "Adjusting to a new environment is just a matter of intelligence". He was right. Mrs Gibson was very happy in Cannington and they stayed at the school for ten years.

Mr Gibson was succeeded by Mr Currie. He was a very poor teacher. The 1969 diary records a visit to see Mr Currie about Stewart and Hamish, but they got no satisfaction. Dad was succeeded as Chairman by Kevin Paterson. Mr Currie and Kevin had a fight at a school Break-up, so Dad had to go back and have another spell as Chairman to get things sorted out again.

Farming Organisations

Dad was one of the founding members of the Cannington YFC. He believed that it was really important for the development of better farming methods. He continued to be an advisor for the Cannington branch for many years. He helped organise the Cannington YFC dog trials until he retired.

Dad was actively involved in Federated Farmers. He would go to the monthly meetings at Cave or Albury with Norman Crawford.

He served on the committee for the Levels Dog Trials and helped with the organisation of their annual trials.

Creek

Down the road from our house, the creek crossed the road through a small ford. Most of the year the ford was dry, but it became a trap for the unsuspecting motorist when the creek was running. Dad would sometimes go down with the tractor and tow someone who had got stuck. I remember one Sunday, when Dad rescued someone in trouble. The man thanked him and said that he would pay him back sometime. Dad said, "You will probably not get a chance to pay me back, but if you show kindness to someone else, and they do the same, it would come around the full circle. There will be a reservoir of kindness waiting for me when I need it". Those words sum up his approach to helping others.

Gran

Dad always took care of his mother. When Uncle Alister and Aunt Shirley were getting married, he arranged for a house to be built for Gran, so that they could live at Riverbank. The foundation for Gran's house was laid in August 1953. Uncle Jack had completed the house by the time of the wedding in the following February. Patricia Casey looked after Alan and me while the wedding was on. Dad shifted Gran's furniture down from Riverbank while they were on their honeymoon.

The hot water was not functioning when she moved in, because Uncle Jack had put in galvanised pipes. The building inspector would not approve the house until copper pipes were installed. She had to go back to Riverbank each day for a couple of weeks to do her washing and have a bath. Gran did her first washing at the new house at the beginning of April.

Uncle Jack also built two hen houses and a workshop across the road. He also put in a large vegetable garden.

In June 1957, Gran cut her foot with the axe while chopping wood. She managed to crawl into the phone and phone Mum. Dad took her to the doctor and she got four stitches. She was more worried about the blood on the hall carpet than her foot, but when they got home, Uncle Jack had already cleaned up the mess. Dad got some crutches, so she was able to walk and continue to look after herself.

We children would drop in each day with a billy of milk when we were biking to school. She would always give us a piece of chocolate and a peppermint out of two jars that she kept on the kitchen bench. We loved going to see her. She had an ostrich egg in her lounge that Uncle Alan had sent back from overseas. We were always fascinated by it.

Gran died quietly in the night on 15 November 1958. Dad wrote the following words

> Very thankful for a loving mother who lived a life of faith and courage. We will all miss her companionship."

On the day of her funeral, he wrote,

> "A day of mixed feelings – sadness of parting with one we loved. Joy of one passing on to a greater life. Thankful for strength and comfort from God and our many friends. A feeling of peace has been upon me these last two days.

At the end of the year he wrote:

> Mother passed away peacefully on 15 Nov, while a gap is left in our lives, I am so thankful she had good health at the end."

Gran was an amazing lady. I remember her as a very kind and peaceful person who was always positive and encouraging. She had a tough life with a lot of sadness. After losing both her husband and son, she could easily have become bitter, but there was no hint on it on her face or in her speech. She always seemed grateful for anything done for and did not expect much. Her faith in God really shone through.

Braeval

The first diary reference to mustering at Braeval was in 1954. Sandy McPherson took his own life in 1958. Dad found him at night, after they had spent the day searching for him. He looked after the place until Jack Dowse was appointed as manager. Dad continued to assist Jack with the mustering. He kept on assisting with the mustering when Hamish McPherson took over after leaving school.

Dad did all of this for nothing, but he also enjoyed the mustering. I think he also felt a bit guilty about not being able to help Sandy. Ruby McPherson had often phoned him, when she was concerned about Sandy. Dad would go up and talk with him. Sandy said that he could feel the hill behind the house pressing down on him like a great weight. Dad would cheer him up and he would feel better for a while, but the depression always came back. Dad felt that as an elder in the church, he should have been more helpful.

Sandy McPherson assisted in solving a nasty robbery. A man held up the people delivering the payroll to the Pareora Freezing works. In those days, all the men at the freezing works were paid in cash, so there was a lot of cash in the payroll. The robber drove over the Pareora Gorge towards Cave, planning to go back to Timaru the other way, but when he got to Martin's Crossing, his stolen car ran out of petrol. He left the car there and started walking towards Cave. Sandy McPherson was looking down with his binoculars and saw the man put a package in the hedge around Gray's house. He was suspicious, so he rang the police. They arrested the man while he was still walking toward Cave. The payroll was recovered from the hedge.

Helping People

Dad and Ellen spent a lot of time helping other people. Here are a few examples from his diary

Robbie Wisely to Hanmer. 1955

Helped Mr Blackmore with crutching. 1955

Helped Uncle Alex to load furniture and move to town. 1957

Took trailer load of wood into Uncle Alex's and boys carted it into the shed for him. 1959

Aunt Cis passed away early in the morning. Went to town to make arrangements for Uncle Alex. 1960

Had doctor for Uncle Jack in the middle of the night. Took him to hospital. 1960

Uncle Jack came home again. 31/8/60

Uncle Jack had a light stoke and had to be taken to hospital. 1961

Ellen spring cleaned Uncle Jack's house before Dad brought him home.

Went to see Jim Paterson on Sunday afternoon. 1962

Collected for Corso. 1962

Took Uncle Alex to hospital. 1962

Uncle Alex died at night. 1965

Bought Uncle Jack home from hospital. 1965

Uncle Jack passed away. Thankful that he passed away so peaceful. 1966

Mrs McPherson passed away in the early morning. Ellen had Diana's wee girls to stay. 1967

Went to church then to hospital to see Jack Kleim. 1968

Auntie Eleanor died. 1968

Went to visit Eddie and Ada at night. 1969

Church

Dad was always involved in the church. When looking back on his youth, he wrote,

> It amazes me when I look back to those days and realise that at that age, I had developed a faith in God. It could only have been through the Bible stories that mother read to us and attending worship in the local school about once a fortnight. I don't remember much of the preaching or what was said, but I know that at that time I reached out to God. I began to talk to him as I went about my work.

> Being the eldest boy in the family, a lot of the responsibility of the farm fell on my shoulders. I began a life of worry. I had all sorts of fears—fears that the farm would not pay, fears that I would not be able to provide for the family.

> Over the years, I became very involved in the church. I did all that one could do in our church - Sunday School teacher, youth leader, manager, elder and later on a lay preacher. I was also very involved in the Young Farmers Club movement and through this, I learned to speak in public and

142

take part in public affairs.

But basically, I was afraid of God. I was scared that he might want me to be a minister and I didn't want to be. I didn't want my dream of having a farm of my own to be interfered with. So, I tried to keep God at a distance. I wanted him to be there if I needed him, but I didn't want him to interfere with my life.

Gran notes in her diary for September 1950 that Dad and Uncle Alister went to the school at night to hear two evangelists speaking.

When Mr Davidson arrived to be minister, he and his wife came for afternoon tea. A few weeks later, Dad showed him around the district. The next year Dad cleaned out Aorangi shearing quarters ready to start a Sunday School. He was the first superintendent. The children would stay in church for the first two hymns. We would walk down the hill, across the road, over the bridge and round the drive to the old Sunday School. A new Sunday School at the bottom of the hill was opened in 1958. We enjoyed having nice warm rooms, but missed the long walk.

We always wore our "best clothes" to church. The girls had dresses that they wore for good. Alan and I had good shirts that we only wore when going out. We always had old clothes under the eiderdown or on our beds. We had to put those on when we came home from school or church. We were not allowed to eat or play until we were changed into our "old clothes".

Mr Davidson died suddenly in 1955. He had been a home missionary and was really good value. Dad went to Christchurch to attend his funeral.

The next minister was Mr Martin. He was Irish, and we found him very hard to understand. I remember him talking about "fillims", when he meant films. He was replaced by Gilbert Hay, a much older man, but great at relating to children. He always carried a bag of pink lollies called "smokers" and gave one to any child he met. The Hays left in 1963.

In 1958, Dad and Alister McKerchar went to Christchurch to attend Stewardship School run by the Presbyterian Church. They organised a stewardship program in the parish. It went well, but unfortunately was focused on getting money. Mum started a women's fellowship that year, as part of the stewardship programme. It eventually became the APW.

Dad was the session clerk for many years. He later represented the church on the PSSA Committee and was active on the committee during the time when the Croft was being built on land donated by the Grant family.

In 1959, I remember going to Chalmers Church in Timaru with Mum and Dad to hear Billy Graham speak via land-line. He was speaking in Christchurch and the sound was carried in live over a telephone line. I was impressed with the technology, as this had not occurred before, but I do not remember his message. This campaign was very successful in New Zealand. Many church leaders became Christians during these meetings. Billy Graham came later in the 1960s, but was not so well received. This time his Auckland meeting was broadcast live on television. That would not happen now.

Dad had always been involved with the Burnett family through their interest in St Davids church. In 1961, Mum and Dad attended the wedding of Catriona Burnett to Richard St Barbe Baker.

The next year Dad was leading a Bible Class. He took the pupils, including Alan, on a visit to Christchurch. They stayed with Mrs McIntosh.

John Allen was inducted in 1964. He was a single man and quite intellectual who really struggled with communicating with farmers. I remember us entertaining ourselves by timing how long he took to do the intimations (notices). The record was 7 minutes. John lived with his mother. She knew lots of people. We sometimes joked that you could name any person in New Zealand and she would know someone who knew them. They left in 1969.

As well as leading Sunday School and Bible Class, Dad was involved in preaching. In 1967, the elders took the service at church, with him preaching the sermon. The next year, he preached a combined service at Albury. Mum wrote that he preached really well. In 1970, she noted that Dad preached really well on Jacob.

The Leggetts arrived in 1969. He did not keep good health, but Mrs Leggett was a lovely person.

Mum was always on the roster for cleaning the church. This was done on a Saturday. She would vacuum the floor, while one of the children dusted all the pews. The person on cleaning was responsible for doing the flowers. Mum would do the arrangement at home and go early on Sunday morning to put in the final touches. During winter, she would do an arrangement with red japonica. It would last for several weeks in the cool church.

Mum collected tea coupons and stamps for the Leprosy Mission. She would clean all the stamps herself, washing them and spreading them out on trays to dry. She was still cleaning stamps when living at Barnes Street.

Dealing with Depression
(Rod)

Dealing with Depression

I'm not sure exactly how it started, but in the late 1950s, I started to get bouts of depression. At first, they only lasted a short time and didn't trouble me too much. But as the years went on the bouts seemed to last longer and to come on more frequently.

During these times, I wouldn't be able to make sensible business decisions. I would put off doing things—which is not good for farming. I was dogged by fear of financial failure. This was crazy because I didn't even have a mortgage on the farm. I had the fear of droughts and floods and all sorts of disasters. I couldn't see anything good in the future. I hated meeting people and used to go out of my way to dodge them. I would cross the street, if I saw someone coming that I knew—I just couldn't bear to talk to them because they appeared to be so happy and inside, I was so miserable.

The things that used to give me so much pleasure—the farm, the animals, the crops and especially my dogs—I now began to hate. Farm work was a chore. The dogs would annoy me so much that I felt like taking a gun and shooting the lot.

I used to dread each day and longed for it to end so I could fall into bed and escape those awful fears. It was strange that I could always sleep, but I'd wake early in the morning with thoughts churning over in my mind. I'd get out of bed and read my Bible and pray, but I found no peace. Some mornings I felt like pulling the blankets up over my head and staying in bed all day. I even thought of selling the farm to escape from this hell.

These were very hard days for Ellen, because I was difficult to live with. When I was in this state of mind, I thought that she would think that I had lost my love for her and would start to resent me. For a number of years, I kept my worries to myself. I didn't even tell her about it. Then the day came when I could no longer face it on my own and I confided in her and she stood faithfully beside me, often spending hours working out our financial system and explaining to me where I was wrong. But I was blind and could see no good in the future.

Eventually, it became so bad that I went to my doctor. What a relief it was when he told me he could do something for me. He put me on a course of pills, one of them being Valium. For a while I seemed better, but then I realised that all that was happening was that I was so dull and dopey that I wasn't really thinking at all. Soon my depression was back.

Great blow

In 1970, when Alan and Ronald were home from school and helping me on the farm, I decided to increase our landholding and bought a further 600 acres in the boys' names. I never discussed with the boys as to whether or not they wanted to be farmers, I just presumed that because I loved farming, they would be the same.

After a few months, Ronald came to me and said he really didn't want to be a farmer. He could see that he was tied up in this farm by what seemed to be a big debt and was afraid that there would be no way out for him. This was a great blow to me. Here I was to be left with twice as much land and only one boy to help me. But I saw my mistake and I released him from the farm and a year later he went to university in Christchurch. While he was there, he had a profound religious experience, receiving the baptism in the Holy Spirit and becoming a very committed Christian. After finishing a degree in economics, he entered Knox College in Dunedin to study for the ministry. We saw a big change in him and Lindsay and we knew that he had discovered something we didn't know about.

One day when he was visiting us, I told him about my problem with depression. It was the first time I had shared this with any member of my family. He showed me from the Bible that I didn't need to be like this and he told me that one thing I shouldn't be taking was pills. So, I took the two bottles of pills and put them in a drawer straight away. I still have them there as a little memorial to what God can do in a man's life.

He prayed for me that day and I experienced a beautiful peace. But without an understanding of the truth behind the feeling, the depression came back again and seemed to get worse than ever. Shortly afterwards we decided to go to Dunedin to visit Ron and Lindsay. I was feeling really bad at this time. Even so, I had a strong feeling that something was going to happen that weekend. I don't know what I thought it might be, because I didn't believe in miracles. In my church, miracles were explained away and even though I believed that God was there, I didn't believe that he could make a difference in my life.

When I told Ron that I had my old problem back again, he was disappointed. He assured me that I shouldn't be like that and suggested that some of his friends could come that night and talk to me. I was so desperate I'd have done anything that he suggested.

That evening as we sat in their lounge, there was a knock on the door. In came what I call a couple young enough to be my own children. I'd expected somebody old, grey-haired and wise to come and here were a couple of kids. I thought to myself, "How crazy can you be!" How could these two help me?

They sensed as soon as they came into the room that fear was my problem and they took their Bibles and began to show me the solution. I realised as they talked that I had never truly believed my sins were forgiven. I was still asking God for forgiveness for sins that I had committed perhaps thirty years earlier. Right there and then I accepted God's full forgiveness. There was a period of confession and I shed a lot of tears. Then they prayed for me and my life was changed.

I came back to the farm a new man. The situation was the same, but I saw things through new eyes. The grass was greener; everything looked better. When I awoke the morning after we arrived home, I heard the birds singing for the first time in years. Of course, the birds had never stopped singing—I just couldn't hear them through my worries. I was so excited to be free from that dreadful depression.

For many years, I had been troubled with pain in my back. I would get a shooting pain down my right leg that almost crippled me. The chiropractor would get me some relief, but it was always temporary. About three months after returning from Dunedin, I realised that I had not had the pain down my leg. It suddenly dawned on me that when God had healed my depression, he had healed that pain from my back at the same time, without me even asking. What a generous God he is. I later had trouble with pain in my neck, but I never had that pain down my leg again.

Spiritual Renewal

Alan Hubbard, an accountant in Timaru, was on the PSSA committee. We often talked together during supper and he told me about a trip through America he had just completed. While waiting at an airport for a delayed plane, he bought a book by David Wilkerson called "The Cross and the Switchblade". He was so impressed with the book, that he bought every copy in the airport bookstore and brought them home to give to his friends. I asked if he had any copies left, because it sounded really interesting. He said that he thought they were all gone, but during the next week, a copy arrived in the mail. The book changed my life. I realised for the first time that there was a life with God that I did not know about.

Sometime later (1969), we noted in the newspaper that a man who had worked with David Wilkerson was speaking in Timaru at the Pentecostal Hall. Mum would not go with me because we had been taught that they were cranks. I was taking Jill back to High School that night, so she agreed to go with me. We decided that we would go a bit late and sneak in the back after the service had started. However, we were met at the door by Charlie Tomlinson, whom I knew through his employment with the Ministry of Agriculture. I was reassured when I saw other men that I knew through farming events, because I knew they were not cranks.

Four teenagers were sitting at the back on bar stools. They pushed and shoved at each other right through the meeting. I thought their behaviour was disrespectful and wondered what would happen to them in our church. However, at the end of the meeting, they all went forward in response to an altar call. I wished I could have gone forward too, but it did not seem to be the right thing for an elder in the church to do. However, this made me even hungrier to know more about God.

Mrs Leggett asked Ellen to pray for a friend who wanted to speak in tongues before she died. She said to ask Lindsay and Ronald, and they would tell her what this meant. Ellen asked Lindsay and she explained about their experience with being baptized in the Spirit.

Sometime later, we arrived down in Dunedin to visit Lindsay and Ronald. I said to them, "I am not going home from here until I receive this baptism in the Spirit". Muri Thompson was in town at the time, so he came around and prayed for us. We both received a glorious touch from the Holy Spirit and went home rejoicing.

Ron had suggested that I should get involved in the Full Gospel Business Mens Fellowship. I did not know anyone involved, so I asked Mrs Leggett and she said she would try to find out. Anyway, I got a phone call the next week inviting me to a meeting. I was a bit shy about going, but Leo Neale had been visiting when the man phoned, so he offered to go with me. That began a great new chapter in my life. I met some wonderful godly men, and they really helped me to grow in my faith. I found great excitement in being with men who believed God, men who pray and see God answer, and I found this fellowship a tremendous boost to my life. As I write this, I'm more excited about Christianity and the power of the risen Jesus and the Holy Spirit than I have ever been in my life.

Ellen got involved in Women's Aglow Fellowship at the same time. She eventually became President of the group in Timaru. She also served on the Area Board. She continued to have fellowship with the Aglow ladies until she moved into the Croft.

Home Meetings

Ellen said to Ronald that she did not feel that she was doing much for God. He suggested that she should get together a group in Cannington and start praying and studying the scriptures and see what would happen. When she had her first meeting, I was all prepared with a study, but only Carol Jean Crawford turned up. She had only been there half an hour when Selwyn phoned and asked her to come home because one of the children was unwell.

Ellen was a bit discouraged, but the next Sunday at church she noted that Jan Tresidder and Heather Harding were present. They lived in Cave and did not come very frequently. Ellen felt the Lord say that these were the people she should ask to the Bible study. She phoned Jan, and she was delighted. She said that she had been hoping that someone would ask her to such a meeting. Jan and Heather both came to the study group and it continued as long as Ellen was on the farm. She continued to have a study group meeting our home while at Barnes St and Church St. The group only finished when we moved into the Croft.

One morning, Jan Tresidder phoned and said that she needed help. I went around and she said that she was being attacked by demons. She was a real mess. I was embarrassed that I was an elder in the church, but did not have a clue what to do. I phoned Charlie Tomlinson and asked him what to do. He phoned back to say that Robert Pullar would see her. I took her in to see him, and as she went into the house, I started back to my car, but Robert said that he wanted me to stay. I did not really want to, but he gave me no choice. Robert prayed in tongues a lot and commanded things to leave. The result was that Jan was really set free and became a new person.

More Change
(Ron)

Family Changes

Jill started training as a nurse at Timaru Hospital in 1969. She lived at the nurse home. The four previous years she had been boarding at Timaru Girls High School. Jean had started boarding at Girls High in 1968. When Stewart started high school in 1970, a better bus service was available to Pleasant Point High School. Mum believed that the school had improved to a good standard, so Stewart and Hamish did not need to go to boarding school.

In 1970, Alan and I both got the mumps and spent several days in bed. Mum was quite worried about us. She kept asking if we were swollen anywhere else, but did not say more.

After five years, I realized that farming was not my scene. After completing University Entrance by correspondence during 1970, I left "Parira" the next year to study at the University of Canterbury.

In January 1971, Jess died. She and Mum had been really close to each other, so Mum was very sad. She had been sick with bowel cancer for quite a while. Mum received $2,300 from her estate.

John Oliver started working for Dad in September 1973. Stewart finished school and started working with Dad in 1974.

Aunty Nell died on 24 March 1977 after getting shingles. Mum wrote in her diary, "We will miss her so much. She was a much-loved Aunt to me. I am pleased that we visited her in February."

Crops

In 1970, we had 16 acres of barley on Highlands. Dad approached the Parris boys as they went contracting with two big Claas headers. These had a 14 ft cutter bar, which had to be towed behind the header when it was on the road. The Parris boys were too busy, so they sent Fergus McFetrich, who was helping them. He arrived at lunchtime and was finished at 6 pm, despite an hour wasted with a blockage. This was a much quicker method of harvesting. The crop yielded 72 bushels per acre, which was a good crop.

We did not have a bulk system. The header loaded the grain into a truck, and another man filled sacks with grain from the back of the truck. They had an electric bag sewer, which sped up the process. Alan and I carted in the 392 bags of sacks of barley.

The next year we had wheat in Eric's Paddock. Fergus got started on the wheat at 12.30 pm and was finished by 6.30 pm. He then started the barley, which was half done when he had to stop. He was finished by 11 am the next day.

What an enormous change. When Dad started farming, harvesting 10 acres of wheat would have been an enormous task. The reaping and binding would have taken a couple of days. Stooking would have taken another two days. Stacking the sheaves would have taken two or more days. Now a similar crop could be harvested in six hours.

New Tractors

In 1970 the old Massey Ferguson was traded in for $1100 on a new MF178 for $4100. The new tractor had multi-power, which enabled it to change to a lower gear ratio without stopping. When pulling an implement up a steep hill, changing gear and getting going again could be quite tricky. The multi-power was a great benefit as the tractor could drop to a lower gear without stopping.

In 1973, Dad brought a second hand Massey Ferguson 35 for $1650, and sold the Fordson for $250. He bought a second-hand MF135 for $4120 in 1977. A year later he traded the MF135 and MF178 for $6000 and bought a new MF188 for $13,000.

Motorbikes

Dad bought his first Honda motorbike in August 1971.

In 1972, he bought another furrow for the plough, converting it into a four-furrow plough. The new tractors were strong enough to pull the larger plough.

The following year, Dad bought another bike, so there was one for each person working on the farm. In 1996, He bought a new Honda for $1220, getting $254 for the old one. He bought a trailer for it the following year.

He bought Arnold Wilson's old Comer truck for $250 in 1973. The gig was sold for $150 in 1976.

Landlords

Once they had more land, Mum and Dad ended up with several houses to rent, but they were too generous to be successful landlords.

Some of the tenants were:

Hamish and Diana McPherson Riverbank. 1964

Bruce Denny Hillview. 1967

Bruce Dick Riverbank. 1969

Colin Ralston Hillview 1970

Sandra Perry Hillview 1972

Valerie and John Coll Riverbank 1972

Sandra Perry Riverbank 1973

John Squire Hillview 1975

Kevin Thompson Riverbank 1975

The Dick family shifted into the Riverbank house in April 1969. They paid $5-00 in advance for two weeks rent. Dad gave them the house free for another two weeks to pay for cleaning it up after vandals. They were always behind in their rent. After they left, Dad found some good copper spouting in the riverbed behind their house. He reported this to the police, but it was never claimed, so he did recoup some of the rent.

155

Highlands

In August 1969, Brian Rolls came to see Dad about Jim Cartwright's farm. After he had looked over it, Alex Cuthbertson rang offering Jock's farm. Dad offered $50,000 to Cartwrights, but the agent came back wanting $62,000. Dad counter offered $56,000 for the farm and offered to negotiate for the stock too. Brian Rolls returned to say that Jim Cartwright was willing to accept $56,000, but wanted $1500 for a paddock of wheat. Brian Rolls rang to say Mr Davies had made an offer on behalf of the Clements. Dad went to town and offered Jim Cartwright $56,000 plus the wheat crop. Jim accepted and the agreement was signed that night. When Alan and Margaret married in 1971, they lived at Highlands.

Retirement

On 17 May 1978, after 33 years farming on Parira, Dad and Mum retired to a house at 39 Barnes Street in Timaru, after Stewart took over the farm. Dad wrote

> I was able to cut myself off completely, selling my dogs and giving up the life I had loved so much. Ellen and I both felt that we would shed tears when we left our home on the farm and shifted into town, but it wasn't like that at all. The Lord blessed us both with a beautiful peace and we came into town to a house where we have been so happy, it is as though we have lived there for years and years.

Mum wrote, "We are very pleased with our home".

The many years of hard work were beginning to take their toll on Mum's body. She had her veins stripped in August 1982. They had troubled her for many years. In September 1987, she went to hospital again to have an operation on her heel and to have her toes straightened.

Dad and Mum continued to lead very busy lives during their retirement. Dad went out to help Stewart on Parira whenever he was required. He continued to kill the sheep and kept both households supplied with meat.

For a number of years, Dad travelled up to Mount Cook Station to assist Donald Burnett with his shearing. He needed someone to help him to get the sheep into the shed and put them out again. I think that Donald also enjoyed his company.

Dad and Mum got really involved at St Stephens church. Both preached quite frequently. Dad was at the door every Sunday welcoming the people. He was an elder and visited everyone in his district every few months. They both made new friends at St Stephens. Dad led a home group that met in the Wilkinson's home.

Dad often assisted the minister by conducting funerals for people he knew. He took church services in various old people homes around the city. He was a frequent visitor at The Croft, where he was later to live.

Mum was on the roster to work at the Goodwill shop and the Trade Aid shop. She continued to be active in Women's Aglow, taking various leadership roles. Many younger women were influenced by her teaching and example. Right until she moved to the Croft, Mum had a group of women meeting in her home for prayer. She became a really good friend with June Barker.

Once every few months, Dad and Mum would do Meals on Wheels. They were on the roster through both the church and the Womens' Division. They continued to do "meals on wheels" after they had moved to Church Street.

Sydney and Melbourne
In November 1981, Dad and Mum took a trip to Sydney with a group of Christians. They would go out on the street at night and

157

sing songs and share the gospel, returning to their hotel room at about 3 am. They also visited the Opera House and travelled to the Blue Mountains.

A few years later, they visited Melbourne to attend a Full Gospel Conference.

Philippines

Dad made two different visits to the Philippines. In November 1980, he went for two weeks with George Meadows and Dick Lewis from Full Gospel. They travelled to Manila via Fiji, Nauru and Guam. When they arrived, they stayed in a hotel in central Manila. For the second week, they stayed with Mr and Mrs Padilla, a millionaire businessman. They visited the McRaes, a New Zealand couple running a home for orphan children.

The team visited several different towns and shared the gospel at many different meetings. On the last Sunday, they preached at a small church in Cabanatuan. It had an iron roof with bamboo walls and slats on the floor. To get there, they travelled through paddy fields where buffaloes were working. The people were incredibly poor. On the day they flew out, they spoke to a meeting of 1500 men in central Manila.

Return Visit to Manila

On the second visit to the Philippines a few years later, Dad went with for a month and travelled with a team from YWAM. He stayed at a YWAM base at a place in Manila called Balut. It was close to a rubbish dump, which is a mountain of plastic and rubbish. The people living there earned money by gathering and selling rubbish. The living conditions were terrible. Most of the people living in the squatter area had come from rural areas, drawn by the hope of work in Manila. The YWAM teams took in food for the children and babies. Dad described their lives in his diary.

> It is incredible the way people have to live, with mud and water everywhere and rubbish of all kind. The people are so thankful for anything you give them. The houses are so small that in NZ, we wouldn't put a dog in them. There is electricity there, but with very crude wiring, no insulation, just wood. In their homes are all sorts of gadgets that they

have recovered from the dump. All the water used in the homes is carried in 20-litre cans, two at a time. It is amazing how clean the people are considering all the mud and slush there is. There are 400 homes in that part of the dump and probably at least 4 people to a home. Old battery cases are used for stepping stones in the mud.

I walked to the top of the dump, where bulldozers are spreading the rubbish and the dump workers are busy picking tins, plastic bags and anything else that they can use. There are little stalls selling drinks and food. They do their cooking on open fires.

Dad's task was to do some maintenance around the base. It had been the home of a wealthy Spaniard, but had become the home for about 50 team members. The house was run down and needed a lot of repairs.

I had to help with some concrete work in the bathroom this morning. I think it will take me a long time to get used to Filipino time. I thought we would never get started, but I am surprised how much we got done. We had to carry the concrete in through the dining room and up the stairs, and through two other rooms and up some steps into the shower. Mary thought it was too hard for me and went and got a Filipino boy to help. I wasn't over-doing it.

It has amazed me how I have got used to living in a hostel with lots of other people. I'm quite used to the conditions now and know the routine. I know where to find cold drinks, ice blocks, tea, coffee, etc. When you think that I have had nearly 70 years of being waited on, one is never too old to adapt to a new way. I believe it is the Lord blessing me and keeping me in peace.

He got an opportunity to share with some of the people living on the dump.

I was asked to lead a bible study among the women from the Dump. I had Mela's wife as an interpreter. I am not sure how good I was, but they seemed to enjoy it. They were a lively group of people. They certainly had the joy of the Lord. It was a lovely experience.

I went with Roberto this morning, first to the hospital and

159

then to the Dump. We met some of the people who had been at my Bible study last night: two at the hospital and two at the dump. Roberto gave me a packet of vitamin tablets and I gave them to the children. He carries a box full of all sorts of pills and drugs, etc. He went to lots of homes to see sick people.

He travelled to Cabanatuan City to visit the family of Zoila, a Philippine girl he had been supporting. It was a long slow trip on crowded buses. Every time they changed buses, they had to make a long walk. They travelled across a large rice-growing plain, with rice paddies stretching for miles. The farmers were working, some planting and others harvesting. He saw people using the wind to separate grain from straw and others drying grain in the sun on the side of the road. The housing was poor. He stayed in a house built on piles over a dirty creek.

He also visited another YWAM base at Cubao City. The climate seemed to be cooler there and the city not so crowded. They visited Malaysia and Singapore on the way home.

Church Street

The house and garden at Barnes Street eventually got too large for Mum and Dad to look after, so they sold the house and bought a new flat. They moved into 119B Church Street on 23 April 1999. The flat had a much smaller garden, but was lovely and sunny. After several years in this flat, Mum was getting crippled by Parkinsons disease and Dad was having difficulty with his eyesight, so they moved into full care at the Croft in 2004. Mum died on 22 Nov 2005 Dad died just six months later on 17 May 2006.

Ellen

Ellen was a good-natured person like her father and nothing seemed to upset her. Her home was always calm and peaceful, a happy place to grow up. If one of the children did something wrong, we would be sent to the bathroom or washhouse, but the worst punishment was her look of disappointment on her face.

She taught her family to be responsible. We were allowed to play outside, in the creek, at the river, up on the cliffs, and the only condition was that the older ones should look after the younger children.

Ellen loved her grandchildren. She remembered all their birthdays and celebrated special events in their lives. When they came to visit, she would put aside her other activities and give them her undivided attention.

Dad said that she was capable in everything that she did. When he came in from working late, the children would be ready for bed, and the meal would be on the table. On Sunday, half an hour after arriving home from church, a roast dinner would be on the table. All she had to do was make the gravy, because the vegetables had been cooking slowly while we were at church. She also provided meals for shearers and harvesters, seemingly without effort.

Ellen worked incredibly hard and she never seemed to rest. Even in the evening she would be darning socks or mending clothes. She poured out her whole life in service to others, never complaining about the hardships that she faced.

Ellen loved people. She spent a lot of time on the phone. If people were in trouble, she would listen. If they were struggling, she would encourage them. She could be the peacemaker when that was required. She always saw the best in people and encouraged rather than criticised. Everyone was treated the same. A farm worker

and a family friend would receive the same welcome. She was gracious and kind to everyone who came to the house.

Ellen loved to make connections with new people. When she met someone for the first time, she would quickly discover someone they both knew or were related to. She had a big heart and there always seem to be room for more people in it.

God was an important part of Ellen's life, right from when she was a young girl. She trusted in him to the end. In between, she spent a lot of time in prayer. She prayed for many people who never realised that she cared about them.

Rod

Rod had dreamed of being a farmer since he was a boy. He fulfilled that dream and became an excellent and innovative farmer. He was especially good at managing livestock and had a natural gift for working with dogs and horses. His approach to farming was that you should leave your farm better than you found it.

Rod applied this principle to the whole of life. When we went on a picnic, he would not just make us pick up our own rubbish, but any rubbish that had been left by other people. We were expected to leave the picnic site better than we found it.

He always worked hard, and he taught his family how to work. He always said, "if a job is worth doing, it is worth doing well".

Rod was always a leader in his community. If there was work to be done, he would be there. If leadership was needed, he was not afraid to put up his hand. He was always respected by those that worked with him.

When he retired, he developed a real gift for caring for people. He visited many people around Timaru, encouraging them and breaking their loneliness.

God was always an important part of Rod's life. His main goal in life was to serve and bless God.

9 780047 348116 2